Prepped

Coming of Age
In Black and White America

A Memoir

D. Veda Pendleton, Ph.D.

First Edition published by KOI Publishing Group 10/2019*

Printed in the United States of America

Copies are available through www.amazon.com.
"I Am From" poem template first designed and developed by Fred First and Jo Carson. Poem content by Veda Pendleton.

Cover photo used with permission from Leslie Baldwin, April 1975 at The Ethel Walker School.
Cover design by Ashley Byland of Redbird Designs.
Book Formatting by Michelle Morrow, www.chellreads.com
Sun graphic used with permission from Creative Commons by Pixabay at www.pixabay.com .
Sundial used with permission from Fiverr at www.fiverr.com .
Photographs of Veda Pendleton taken 1972-1975 in Simsbury, Connecticut.

Library of Congress Cataloguing-in-Publication Data

Pendleton, D. Veda

Prepped: Coming of Age in Black and White America

1. Prep school 2. Preparatory school 3. memoir 4. Gifted education 5. Black students in prep school 6. Black girls 7. College prep 8. Young adult memoir 9. The Ethel Walker School 10. Simsbury, CT 11. Pine Bluff, AR

ISBN-13:978-1729688335

ISBN-10: 1729688330

Dedication

To all of the children of color whose giftedness, talents, and purposes have not yet been discovered…keep your head to the sky! Always know that your life has meaning, purpose, and value. You are enough!

To the Sensational Seven (Kaleb, Olivia, Isaiah, Elijah, Lauren, Gabrielle, and Rachel) who come for Cousins Camp…I will always love you and will work for the best for you, your future cousins, and children everywhere.

To the memory of my dear friend, LaMerril John Sims, (January 11, 1957 – September 22, 2019) – A friend loves at all times.

Author's Note

This book is based on the author's memories of events from the 1970's. The names and other identifying traits of some individuals have been changed to protect their privacy. This work has been reconstructed to the best of the author's memory in order to tell her story.

Table of Contents

Acknowledgements

I have never done anything completely by myself. Even in birth, my mother was there. This work is no exception to that fact. A lot of people helped to make this story possible. These individuals contributed to my story. I am grateful.

This debt of love I owe to my family from which I was created and the family that I created; and to Doris Pendleton, LaWanda Pendleton, Marion Humphrey, André Pendleton, Dr. Marian Higgins, Lauren McClain, Nyoka Delphina Browno Woods, Lucy Rapp, Gabi Coatsworth, Lis Harris, Charita Cole Brown and Demi Hunter, Kathy Mansfield, Anne Greene and the staff at Wesleyan Writer's Conference 2018, A Better Chance, Inc, Dr. Bonnie MacDougall, Jacqueline Kashkoush, Judy Laning, Tara Kelly, Allana Thompkins and Ricky Theo, Diane White, Dr. Kimberly Mucker-Johnson, Dr. Renée Campbell and Mrs. Mary Campbell, Nancy Pollock, Sarah and Ray Grant, Lynn Lexime, Marion Paterson, Brenda Watson, Adrian Layne, Nicole Finley, Dr. Joy Lawson Davis, Dr. Dode Washington, Joan Countryman, Leslie Baldwin, Nancy Stearns, Kelvin Bryant, Jürgen Tossman, Veronica Wright, Saundra Hamon, Dr. Stephen A. Broughton, Gail Hollaman, Pamela Fletcher Porter, Betty Bailey, Retired

Major Benjamin Frazier, Any Good Thing Writing Challenge, my cheerleaders at Greenwood—you know who you are, and all of my friends who encouraged me along *this* journey. Many of these individuals read various drafts of my work and gave meaningful feedback. Thank you.

To God be the glory! He keeps on doing great things for me.

Foreword

In 1972, the first hand-held scientific calculators sold for $395 and gasoline was fifty-five cents a gallon. Motown released Michael Jackson's debut album *Got to be There,* with hit songs, "Ain't No Sunshine" and "Rockin' Robin" in January. In June, five men were arrested for burglary at the Watergate offices of the Democratic National Committee. In the fall of that year, Veda Pendleton, age fifteen, an African American student from Pine Bluff, Arkansas, entered Ethel Walker School, a girls' boarding school in Simsbury, Connecticut.

Veda Pendleton's experience with school integration had begun four years earlier when she was in sixth grade; the local school district had set up a teacher exchange between some of the all-black and all-white schools in the city. The next step in the city's compliance with desegregation orders was a "freedom of choice" program, which allowed her to enroll in seventh grade at Trice Junior High School where she met black students from different neighborhoods and studied with white students for the first time. With integration of the Pine Bluff public schools in 1970, black and white students attended school together under court order. While the city did not experience demonstrations or violence, there were threats. "There's been a bomb threat. Please evacuate the building," the intercom announced at least once a week at Southeast Junior High School where Veda attended eighth grade. Previously, an all-black school for students in grades – seven through twelve, the building now included white teachers and white students, with the white folks acting as if they were better than the blacks. Although she was enrolled in advanced English and mathematics classes, Veda noted right away, not only that black students were very much in the minority, but also that white teachers had low expectations for these students and made no effort to support them when it was clear that a particular student was at a disadvantage. Hence, with each grading period, Veda's advanced classes lost more and more black students.

> "My family was aware of the challenges that black people faced in America, particularly in the South, and they wanted me to be able to compete with the best of them and to transcend my circumstances," she writes. "They wanted me to be able to use my brain and the teachings they had given me to overcome some of the racial challenges and struggles that black people face in America, and so they prepped me before I ever considered going to prep school."

By attending Ethel Walker School, Veda was following the footsteps of her cousin Marion, who six years earlier had gone off to Exeter, then Princeton University; he was now actively recruiting other black students for the A Better Chance (ABC) program. *Prepped* is Veda Pendleton's account of her journey through the program of a New England prep school in the mid-1970s. It's a story of learning to live in a world where the familiar changes places with the strange. It's a story of learning what Langston Hughes called "The Ways of White Folks" in a world of roommates and uniforms, of college preparatory courses, sports classes dressed in tunics and bloomers, of dances at boys' schools, and "slave auction" fundraisers. It's a story of mixed expectations in a "meritocracy" that hadn't gotten around to recognizing its own biases.

The young woman who arrived on the campus of The Ethel Walker School in 1972 was prepared, with her family's help, to see herself as a thinker and a problem solver, capable of meeting the challenges that America presents to people of color. While her journey began with a three-week ABC summer program at Williams College in Massachusetts, designed as an introduction to life in a diverse community, the school that she entered in the fall had few black students, and all the adults were white. Navigating a world where they rarely saw themselves, in the classroom, on the screen, in the books they read, or the curriculum in general, was a burden that students of color carried for decades in the post Brown v. Board of Education era of American primary and secondary education. Veda Pendleton's memoir traces her growth during her three years at Walker's before going on to college. It tells how she came to understand and appreciate, if not to embrace, that world of difference.

Joan Countryman, August 2019
Consultant and Founding Head,
The Oprah Winfrey Leadership Academy for Girls in South Africa

I Am From – Part I

I am from a sizzling hot comb and curling iron, a back porch, and wringer washer...

...from Hair-rep, thick green Prell, Dutch Cleanser, and Pine-Sol.

I am from the paint-bare house and the new one, too...

...paneled, tiled, and smelling new

I am from irises, gardenia bushes, philodendrons, honeysuckle, plum, pecan, and chinaberry trees...

...blooming in the yard with scents flowing in the breeze.

I'm from Christmas, Easter, and Mother's Day speeches and church meetings with pressed hair, under slips, petticoats, white lace socks, and patent leather shoes...

...from Rosie and James and Jimmie and Doris.

I'm from the truth telling, the faith-filled, and the strong-willed...

...from "always do your best and let God do the rest."

I'm from the mourner's bench at St. Paul Church, labor unions, picket lines with picket signs on a scorching 4th of July.

I'm from East Harding and East 19th Avenues in Pine Bluff, Arkansas City, and McGehee, too…

…purple hull peas, turnip greens, burnt candied sweet potatoes, skillet cornbread, pound cake, fried chicken, and sweet potato pies to boot.

I am from the Trail of Tears across south Georgia, Alabama, and Mississippi, that James, Benjamin, and Priscilla walked…

…from the letter writing, politics entering, and campaign-winning…

…photographed and archived on a love wall and a family wall with everyone grinning…

…pictures remembering and honoring the lives of mothers, fathers, sisters, brothers, and all y'all.

1

The Letter

A mysterious letter arrived at my new home in Louisville, KY, in April 2007. The handwriting on the ecru colored envelope looked familiar, but I couldn't remember when or where I had last seen it. The penmanship was evidence of someone who took great pride in communicating well on handwritten notes. The return address was unfamiliar and indicated that the sender lived in a New England state in a town with a curious name. I had no clue who the sender might be. Before my curiosity could get the best of me, I quickly tore open the envelope. It read:

> Dear Veda,
>
> I have been working with a search firm for several years, and I assisted with the recent search for the Head of School position at The Ethel Walker School. I saw your application and knew that you had to be my Veda from Walker's long ago. I hope that you are. You might remember me as Martha Levy, but I am now Martha Lehmann. If you are my Veda, here is how you can contact me."
>
> Sincerely,
>
> Martha Lehmann

I sighed a deep sigh. First, I knew that the search had concluded without as much as a telephone call to me from the search committee. I had applied for the position at my *alma mater* in hopes that I would be a viable candidate, but that did not happen. One of my classmates was on the search committee, but she too found no reason for at least a telephone interview. I knew I was credentialed beyond what was necessary to head such a school, having served as a university department chair and as a college dean, but still that was not enough to pique the interest of the search committee.

Secondly, the sigh was for the surprise in receiving a letter from Martha Levy, one of my English teachers at The Ethel Walker School in the 1970's. For years since the advent of the Internet, I had googled her name hoping to reconnect with her even though I was never really sure why I wanted to get in touch with her. Perhaps I wanted to tell her about my life since our time together at Walker's, about my schooling, about my family, my children, grandchildren and past relationships. Maybe I just wanted to see how she and her son were doing. He'd had a crush on me when he was nine and I was fifteen. Perhaps I wanted her to be proud of me and what I had accomplished. Maybe, I wanted to let her know that my preparation at Walker's had been worth the struggle, the effort and the change in me.

In any case, Mrs. Levy had found me. I read the words "my Veda" several times, wondering why she had referred to me with such endearment. Of all my memories of our time together at Walker's, I never felt she liked me or even wanted to get to know me but saying "my Veda" demonstrated a fondness on some level. Could this be the same woman?

I wondered what she had been doing since she had left Walker's. Now, I had an opportunity to find out. I emailed her. It was the beginning of reunion and much needed redemption.

***

I was the first black female student of my generation from Arkansas to earn a scholarship to attend a prep school. All the other scholarship recipients of the 1970's were males. It would be decades before another black female from Arkansas would attend a boarding school. My venture to a place like Walker's was rare. When I decided to apply and subsequently attend Walker's, I had no clue that I was the first or the only black female to do so. It was the beginning of my time as a lonely only with tremendous personal growth.

2

827 East Harding Avenue

Jimmie and Doris Pendleton rented our home at 827 East
Harding Avenue in Pine Bluff, Arkansas, for $25 a
month. Two sisters rearing their children together, they
moved to this address a few days after my birth. Doris was
the older of the two, but Jimmie was more outspoken.
Jimmie was my mother, and she was the tough one. No one
got away with any lie or injustice. If you lied to her, you
were immediately held accountable for your offense. Aunt
Doris for whom I was named had a gentler touch. She used
nicer words and was more diplomatic in her conversations.
While listeners thought they were dealing with the nicer
sister, Aunt Doris, whom we called Dollee, always came
away with what she wanted. She just used different words
and was more tactful.

Jimmie's children called her by her first name. As
toddlers, Buster and I had attempted to say some version of
"mother" when talking to her, but it always came out as
"muh" which she despised. One day she finally told us if we

couldn't say "mother" just call her Jimmie. That's what we did.

East Harding, the busiest street in town, carried traffic in and out of the city. Where Harding Avenue ended, Highway 65 South began and took folks down a road lined with cotton, soybean and irrigated rice fields to more rural communities in southeastern Arkansas, northern Louisiana and parts of western Mississippi. Our house at 827 was a rental poorly maintained by our slumlord, a local realtor. The house sat on concrete blocks on a corner lot at Harding Avenue and Virginia Street and was partially painted white. Because it sat so high off the ground, many of our rubber balls became silhouettes under the house, because we were too frightened of snakes, bugs and other creatures to crawl underneath to retrieve them.

The faded white paint on the house had cracked and peeled so badly that it looked as though someone had scraped the paint off in preparation for re-painting but neglected to do so. It was a forgotten house. The slumlord never bothered to re-paint it. It was not insulated, and pest control was not a priority. A neighbor cut our grass for 25¢ every two weeks and trimmed the hedges. The pecan and chinaberry trees in our yard were never pruned. The garage on the property leaned to one side, was always dark and damp, and was a forbidden place for us to play or explore.

We relied on window fans during the hot Arkansas summers, and open flame natural gas space heaters in winter. Inside the house, the wallpaper peeled off the walls, and my brother Buster and I helped to remove much of it. When the owner re-papered the walls, he used cheap glue and the paper puckered and sagged heavily off the walls and ceilings like a balloon filled with water about to burst. Later, Buster or I stuck a finger through the sagging paper only to find an air pocket and cold air. The only thing between the wallpaper and the outside was shiplap used to form the walls.

827 was a five-room house with porches on the front and the back. Buster and I sat on our front porch and watched the cars from every state go by. During summer months, we looked to see how many out-of-state license plates we could identify. Sitting on the wooden planks, we waved and spoke to everyone who walked past our house. At night, after taking our baths, we returned to sit on the front porch fanning and slapping mosquitoes and trying to catch fireflies.

Once inside the house and getting ready for bed, Jimmie used a spray pump to send a heavy mist of Black Flag into the air to kill flying mosquitoes in our bedroom. We survived breathing those fumes while sleeping because the windows were raised, but a raised window also meant more mosquitoes entered through the holey window screens. Itchy mosquito bites were the order for every spring and summer day. I was careful not to scratch my bites because I didn't want dark spots and scratches on my legs like I had seen on other kids at school. My grandmother's remedy of applying Campho-Phenique, when we had some, took the itch out of the mosquito bites.

One year our family got a yellow and white metal glider and two metal chairs for the front porch. We thought we had arrived when that porch furniture was delivered because then we could sit up higher like our neighbors and have a better view of the passersby.

Buster, my younger brother whose given name is James André, and I slept with Jimmie in a back room of the house. Our room had a full-sized bed, and a chifferobe held our clothing. We didn't have many clothes, but what we had was always clean. Jimmie worked at a dry cleaner and laundry business when we were young. She walked to and from work every day, and during her lunch breaks, washed and ironed our clothes. Buster and I joked that we had itchy rashes on our necks from rubbing them on the starched collars of our shirts.

Dollee and her only child, Marion, slept in twin beds in a bedroom at the front of the house. For years, they shared the same space. Marion is nicknamed Brother because when he came into the world, he was a brother to my sister LaWanda. She was the first born of our generation, and she slept in what would have been a dining room directly behind the living room. She was the only one with bedroom furniture that included a bed, a dresser, and a chest of drawers.

Our kitchen held a metal kitchen table and pewter-colored vinyl upholstered chairs, a sink, and a stove. Off from the kitchen was the screened back porch, which served as a laundry room with a wringer-type washer. Sheets, towels, and underwear were washed there and hung with wooden clothespins on the clothesline in the yard under the chinaberry tree. Those sheets and towels always held a fresh, natural scent.

After a few years, the washer stopped working, and Buster's red Radio Flyer wagon, a Christmas gift, quickly became the transport for underwear, sheets, and towels to the local laundromat at 13th Avenue and Missouri Street. It was walking distance from our home, and we made weekly trips to the laundromat as Buster and I fussed over taking turns pulling the load. Our laundry was tucked safely inside pillowcases and placed in plastic baskets. We stuffed an orange and blue box of Tide in the side of the wagon and were extra careful not to tip over the wagon and spill the detergent.

It cost fifteen cents to wash a load of clothes and ten cents for a drying cycle. Dimes and nickels were precious, and Jimmie and Dollee fussed when the clothes were not dry after two cycles. That meant more dimes. They complained when the owner changed the timing on the dryers to make more money.

We were a poor family, in terms of dollars and cents, but our lives were enriched in many ways. Although the slumlord neglected general maintenance of our house, we took great care to maintain our home. We had to care for what we had.

Dollee was the first in our family to graduate from high school. Mama, my maternal grandmother, and Papa, my maternal grandfather, had not been so fortunate. Papa was born in 1861, four years before the end of slavery in America. His family left Georgia on foot when he was a youngster headed for Arkansas. Mama was born in 1894 in a small community in southeastern Arkansas, and like others of her day, she worked in the cotton fields and homes of white landowners. Mama was a York on her mother's side, and the year she was born, thirty-two members of the York family died, including Mama's mother, Susie York. The Yorktown community in southeast Arkansas is named for her family. Mama's daddy was Andy Drew, and he later married a woman who was not nice to Mama when she was a child. It took Mama a long time to forgive that woman, and Mama carried with her the fear of child abuse and neglect for other children into her dotage. She was always concerned about how babies and young children were treated. She never wanted to see a child mistreated by an adult, and so, she made it her business to help where and whenever she could with the young in our family.

Black love is our wealth and most white biographers will never understand that fact about black people. That's the wealth we had, and it's that love which has held us together and helped us face—with courage—uncertain economic days over the years. In addition to family love, our lives were rooted in the black Baptist church and everything that the church symbolized. Our faith family was our community family among the women and men there who held high expectations for us, even when there was no evidence we would amount to anything. They believed in us long before we learned how to believe in ourselves as they recognized our giftedness and talents, even when others did not. It was the push from home and the support of the black church community that propelled us to seek greater opportunities. Their love prepped us for the life that was to come.

At St. Paul Church, two offerings were taken each Sunday: one for tithes and offerings and the other for missions, both home and foreign. The offerings for home missions went to needy families in our community, and our own family was a recipient of that benevolence. As a child, I was unaware of the offerings that landed on our doorstep. I just thought our deacons were checking on us as congregants. We were truly economically disadvantaged, but we had all of the other supports that children and families need to grow and to thrive. For that, I am eternally grateful.

We had love and togetherness. We had protection and safety. We had patience and kindness, especially kind words. Jimmie and Dollee first told me they loved me and that I was beautiful. We had instruction on life tasks, like cooking, mowing grass, cleaning, and ironing. We had correction and discipline in word and action. We had admonitions like, "You will always have to be twice as good as the white students to get half the chance they get. You have to be better." That lesson was taught at home and at church. And we had lessons on how to love and to look out and care for each other.

We had lessons in civility and the true meaning of "*Do unto others as you would have them do unto you.*" Lastly, we had nourishment with both natural food and with the Word of God. We had what we needed to help us grow physically, emotionally, and spiritually.

The ideals that my family instilled in us gave us something on the inside that would sustain us on the outside and help us become the persons they felt we could become. And each of us did her or his best. We were prepared for whatever the world offered us before we were aware of that preparation or that we even needed it.

***

Large stretches of East Harding had no traffic lights. When car brakes squealed, it usually meant a car crash. If there was no sound of crashing metal, it was much worse. Several times, a child was struck by a car while attempting to cross Harding.

By the time Buster and I were allowed to come out the front door, neighborhood women had covered the child's body with a white sheet. We witnessed death right in front of us.

Jimmie put the fear of God in us about crossing the street. After teaching us how to look both ways for oncoming traffic, she said, "If you get hit by a car, I'm gonna kill you."

We didn't want her to kill us, so we paid close attention when crossing any street, especially Harding. Jimmie said what she needed to say to get the gravity of her point across and to protect us. It worked.

3

Prepped for What? – Part I

My mother and Dollee instilled a spirit of excellence in each of us. Although we didn't have much, we had to keep clean the things that we did have. My job on Saturday mornings was to dust the furniture. I never liked dusting, but I knew that it was necessary. Dollee always checked my work to see if I had done it correctly.

When I was nine, LaWanda left home for her job in New York as a dietitian, and I became the family cook. I had to start dinner every afternoon after school before Dollee got home. I resisted at times because I wanted to play outside, but she insisted I learn how to cook the right way. When making a dish, if she said the onions, peppers, and celery had to be minced, by golly, they had to be minced, or else I had to re-do it. Chopped was not good enough, if the recipe called for minced. By her side, I learned how to make homemade yeast rolls, pies, German chocolate cakes, and pound cakes. Presentation was important to her in cooking, and she made sure that the food that we prepared looked visually inviting and tantalized the taste buds. Dollee showed me how to put care and love in my meals by thinking about the presentation. Sunday dinner was prepared on Saturday nights, and that's when I learned how to cook. Dollee prepared me to provide nutritious meals for my family with love.

On Saturday afternoons, before wrestling came on television, Jimmie taught me how to iron clothes. She shared with me what she knew how to do best. I learned how to starch (she made her own starch from scratch) and iron a shirt almost to perfection. She said, "See, you iron the cuffs and sleeves first. Then you iron the collar and the shoulders. The last parts to iron are the flat panels on the front and the back." It was important for me to spend learning time with Jimmie to bond with her and to understand that she had something of value to teach me.

Although Jimmie wore short hair, hair care was important to her and the other community women. After Saturday ironing, she straightened hair. Three women came to our house to get their hair hot combed for fifty cents or pressed and curled for a dollar-fifty. They discussed current events and church news, while Jimmie pressed and curled their hair.

In the 1970's, several black children in our community took piano lessons. Our black families believed that young children needed to take piano lessons in order to be cultured, to know music, and to have a musical talent that could possibly become a source of income for them. It was what black families did for their children to help them become accomplished learners and musicians. My family was no different, and Sister Ora, one of my mother's older half-sisters, insisted I be the one in our family to take piano lessons. Sister Ora was married to Brother Josh White. They were called "Sister" and "Brother" because they were so much older than my mother and aunt, and that was their way of showing respect to their elders, a carryover from our African heritage which demanded respect be shown to elders, even if the elder person was a sibling.

Mr. Henry Moore was a music professor and classical clarinetist at Arkansas AM&N (Agriculture, Mechanical, and Normal) College in Pine Bluff, the only public historically black college in Arkansas. Mr. Moore began offering piano lessons to community black children in the summer of 1966. On Tuesday afternoons, he picked up Nick Thomas, a neighborhood friend, and me in his yellow Volkswagen Beetle and drove us to the campus for our lessons. My half-hour lesson was fifty cents.

Eventually, I traveled to the college campus on my own via the local city bus for my piano lesson. I walked from our house up the street to the bus stop at Harding and Missouri Street to catch the bus. I rode the bus to the north side of town, made appropriate transfers, disembarked the bus, and walked the three blocks to the campus alone.

Jimmie was a human GPS. Sharing her sense of direction, she taught me the layout of the city streets. She told me that the streets located east of Main Street were named after states and ran north and south. The streets located west of Main Street were named after trees. She also told me that the intersecting numbered streets ran east and west and were called avenues. East Harding, however, was named after a former U.S. president. Jimmie carried a folded three-by-five card which displayed the layout of the city streets. That card gave me a visual for traveling in Pine Bluff.

Armed with her visual, I traversed the city on the local bus alone. I had ridden the bus before with family members, but never by myself. Black people could finally sit wherever they wanted on the bus, so I sat near the driver at the front. If the bus was crowded with blacks, or the only seat left was one next to a black person, whites who boarded the bus stood instead of taking a seat beside one of us.

The only fear I had in traveling alone was my fear of dogs. I don't remember worrying about being harmed physically by other humans. Walking the three blocks, I was keenly aware of the places where dogs lived outside. Unless I heard a dog barking or a chain rattling, I strutted with confidence, carrying my John Thompson piano book under my arm. The fifty cents for my lesson and my fifteen cents return bus fare were neatly tied in a floral cotton handkerchief and tucked into my sock for safe keeping.

Through my piano lessons, I learned to read music and about fractions with whole notes, half notes, quarter notes, and eighth notes. I also studied the language of music and Italian terms common to musicians such as *piano, forte, staccato, pianissimo, adagio,* and *largo.*

Piano practice was a must. At first, we did not own a piano. After school, I walked six blocks to Sister Ora's house and practiced on the piano in her living room. She did not play the piano, but she always knew when I made a mistake and made me play the tune again. If Brother Josh was home, he agreed with her and encouraged me to try harder.

In November 1966, I received a piano for my December birthday and Christmas gift. Although it was a big present, at ten years of age, it just didn't seem like the right gift for me at that time. I didn't understand or fully know how to appreciate such a purchase by Jimmie and Dollee. My other present that year was a basketball. I didn't understand that, either, since I didn't play basketball or have a basketball goal. I no longer had an excuse for not being able to practice the piano.

Not long after receiving the piano, and when I could play two hymns, I became the youth pianist for our Sunday school. Every second Sunday of the month, I had to play the piano at church. Dollee was the Sunday school superintendent, and she insisted on my playing for the church. Initially, I played only the melody in the treble clef with my right hand. That was enough for Dollee and other Sunday school workers, who pushed and encouraged me. Although other church musicians were paid a small sum, Jimmie forbade me to accept any monetary compensation. She said I was serving the Lord, and no pay was expected. It was my reasonable service. Dollee agreed. That's how my family gave back to our church community and instilled in us the concept of serving.

Although Jimmie spent many of her working years at laundry and dry-cleaning businesses, she spent several years working as a sander at a furniture manufacturing company. Every day, she stood and sanded wood to be made into bed frames. I still remember one of those evenings when she arrived home, having gotten a ride from someone at work. When she rounded the car to cross Harding Avenue, I didn't recognize her at all. Her rich, chocolate skin was covered in barley-colored fine sawdust. It seems that on previous days, she had washed most of the sawdust off before she left her workplace. That day, she had not, and I quietly wept for my mother. With a child's heart, I knew she worked hard in order to provide for us. I knew that if the sawdust was covering her face, there had to be sawdust in her hair, eyes, ears, mouth, and lungs. I vowed that day that I would not do that kind of work. Don't get me wrong; there is dignity in all work, but I knew my mother deserved better opportunities than what she had experienced. I had to seek different paths through reading, writing, and learning at its best.

Jimmie's abilities were not lost behind that sawdust. She joined the United Furniture Workers of America local union and soon after became the president of the chapter on her job. Because she resented unfair labor practices, she became an activist involved with the AFL-CIO, the local chapter of the NAACP, and the A. Philip Randolph Institute.

A few months into her tenure as union president, she led an 18-month strike against the company. Under her leadership, she organized workers to walk the picket lines and provided workers with food stamps and other vouchers to help them stay afloat during the strike. When workers did not show up to walk the picket lines, Buster and I took shifts. Since no one wanted to give up their holiday celebrations on the Fourth of July that year, Buster and I stayed on the picket line the entire day. And because I had reading and math skills, I managed the union's checkbook and wrote checks to members for support during the strike. Unofficially, I served as secretary and treasurer because my mother didn't trust anyone else. She knew I could, and she made sure I did it right.

***

With all these activities at 827 East Harding, what was I being prepped to do or to become? What was I supposed to make of myself as a child, a young girl, a learner? How were the skills I learned at home to be put to use in my world and in the larger society as a whole? What I learned at home were my funds of knowledge, upon which all other learning would be built. I was prepped for school and future academic pursuits at home with my economically disadvantaged black family and community.

My family was aware of the challenges black people faced in America, particularly in the South, and they wanted me to be able to compete with the best of them and to transcend my circumstances. They wanted me to be able to use my brain and the teachings they had given me to overcome some of the racial challenges and struggles that black people face in America, and so, they prepped me before I ever considered going to prep school. I was prepared for learning and thriving to the best of my family's ability and to be civil in society. I was prepped to be a survivor and a warrior. Their instruction was not by accident; it was all-intentional.

4

/me-ander-ING/

eandering. It was the first word I came across as an avid reader that I could not readily pronounce. In fifth grade, the word stumped me and my reading buddy. I had not heard or read the word before. No one in my family had ever used it, I had not heard the word used on the evening news, nor read it in the newspaper, and my teacher had never used it. So, how was I supposed to know this word on sight? My reading buddy and I read aloud to the teacher all year, and she allowed us to read as far as we could in the time allotted or until we came to a word we could not pronounce correctly. *Meandering* stopped us, and for whatever reason, neither of us bothered to look up the pronunciation in a dictionary.

I entered first grade a reader. Buster and I attended a pre-school at Allen Temple African Methodist Episcopal Church, our only formal instruction before first grade. Only a half-day program, parents had the option of sending their first-grade child to either the morning or afternoon session. My mother put me in the morning session, but I sometimes stayed for the afternoon, as well. After all, had I not stayed, I was going to have to walk the three blocks home by myself, let myself in the house, and wait for Wanda or Dollee to get home. I didn't have sense enough at six years old to be afraid of either walking home or being at home alone. My mother and aunt adequately warned me about stranger dangers and dared me to answer the door, but I was a precocious child and wanted to learn as much as I could, as fast as I could learn it.

I was a good reader. Much of my literacy development was centered around the church and learning to recite verses from the Bible. Dollee read the Bible to Buster and me every morning before we went to pre-school, and later, to elementary school. On special days recognized by our church, I recited short poems called "speeches" in front of Sunday school audiences. We practiced those speeches for weeks to perfection, under the guidance of parents and other capable teens and adults, with the right vocal tones and exact pronunciations of words. Literacy impacted my early development.

I was also the student who was the chosen "*show off*." I wasn't showing off, but whenever our school had visitors in our classroom, I was usually the one chosen to read for them. When black school district leaders like Mrs. Maylene Arrant came to check on the progress of the Negro students in our segregated school, I read for them so my performance became an indicator to the leaders that we were making adequate progress in learning and that the black teachers were indeed doing their jobs. Although a few others were sometimes chosen to read, I never paused to think about my other classmates, who were never asked to read for visitors. In my childhood world, all that mattered was that *I* got to read and to learn.

I liked helping and pleasing others. In school, that meant I worked hard to please my teachers, and based on their approval, I determined how I would feel about myself as a learner. I aimed to please my mother first, then my teachers. I was not going to make some gross error that would unnecessarily summon my mother to school. My desire to please also led me down the path of perfection and of always wanting to get the right answer. I wanted to have the best work possible, and I was willing to work hard to achieve that goal.

My reading ability allowed me to sail through most of elementary school with ease. I read everything. There were few books in our school during my first two years. We did not have a school library. Our teachers owned the books we read, and with the exception of the set of *World Book* encyclopedias, I did not have a home library. I did not own *any* books, but I fell in love with reading. In third grade, we got a school library and a black male librarian, but by that time, I was already taking bi-weekly jaunts to the Jefferson County Public Library downtown to check out books.

Our family did not own a car, so I rode the local city bus downtown and walked to the public library. The librarian began to expect my arrival and soon pointed me in the direction of books she thought might be of interest to me. I read lots of books by Beverly Cleary and later moved to biographies of Eleanor Roosevelt, George Washington Carver, John F. Kennedy, and Mary McLeod Bethune. Biography and realistic fiction were my favorite literary genres.

I sometimes shudder now as I think about my forty-eight pound frame walking alone on the street in the second largest town in Arkansas at the time. My mother and aunt expected me to know and to do the right thing, no matter what. I felt the same way about myself. I believed I could do whatever I needed to do, and so I did it. Little did I know how far that disposition would take me in life.

After a few days of guessing how to pronounce "meandering," one of us pronounced it correctly, and other than learning how to play checkers, that is all that I remember learning in fifth grade. That year, our teacher knitted, played checkers, and snacked all day from her seat. And while she was nice to us, it became apparent that she had already retired from teaching us. Some days, she would even send a student to Rich's, the local burger drive-in, to get her an ice cream parfait. To get to the fast food joint, we had to leave the school campus and cross East Harding Avenue. I can only imagine what would have happened had one of us been kidnapped, assaulted, or struck by a car on the way, but no one ever got hurt. Our teacher continued that practice long after I left the school.

Sixth grade was a different matter. Schools in the South had been ordered to desegregate, but no one was clear about what that process would be. In 1968, Pine Bluff School District leaders decided to integrate our schools with a teacher exchange prior to the students' arrival. Three teachers from our all-black school went to an all-white school, and three white teachers from an all-white school came to our all-black school. Two of those white teachers hold special memories for me. Mrs. Welch was a first-grade teacher. She was a nice white lady with dark hair, who smiled a lot. She and my teacher decided I would be a good helper for her after I had completed my schoolwork. Although I began teaching Sunday school at age nine, this was my first foray into public school teaching. I became a teacher's helper and worked with a small group of students. The other white teacher I remember fondly was Mrs.

Hatcher, my homeroom teacher. Our teachers decided to allow us to switch classes for different subjects. Mrs. Hatcher taught reading and science, Mr. Smith taught geometry, and Mrs. Taylor taught social studies. I grew as a reader and learner. Mrs. Hatcher brought SRA reading cards, and we read them and answered the questions on the back. The content on the cards was mostly non-fiction, which I had never been challenged to read independently. Reading non-fiction was for learning science and social studies in school and reading the newspaper.

When I found myself struggling with reading for the first time, Mrs. Hatcher was there to help me and the members of my advanced reading group comprehend non-fiction passages. I wanted to resist at first, but I also wanted to see how much more I could learn. This nice white lady intrigued me. She didn't look like me, but she cared enough to make me a better reader, and she was patient and willing to spend time with me to make sure I had what I needed to be successful in school and beyond. She took time with us to ensure that we learned grade level content. We read an excerpt from the *Kon-Tiki* (which I didn't understand) and had to memorize the poem, *My Shadow* by Robert Louis Stevenson.

What was most impressive about Mrs. Hatcher was the way she valued us as human beings. Her white skin did not matter and neither did our black skin. What mattered most was that she thought of us as human beings with gifts from God which she was charged to nurture and to grow within each of us. We were her students, and she was our teacher, and we were going to learn while we were in her room. And learn we did. She taught us how to understand and how to know when we were achieving academically. If we were taking away new knowledge in ways that were meaningful to us, learning was taking place; otherwise, we were marking time.

Mr. Smith, a black man, who was also new to our school, taught us mathematics. A passionate mathematician, he made us think that we were great mathematicians, too. Because of his teaching style, I really thought I had a handle on geometry, only to find out later that I did not. He made sure we understood what he taught. When one of us didn't get it one way, he changed course and taught it a different way or used different language that helped us understand. He differentiated his instruction to meet the learning needs of his students. He met us where we were, used our background knowledge, and took us where we needed to be. We used manipulatives, and I got my first compass and protractor for his class. Mr. Smith believed in us and worked to help us master math concepts. He was our math hero.

***

"Where are you going to school next year?" was asked over and over again. We wanted to know where each of our classmates was going to go to school after sixth grade. In the spring of 1969, I had to decide where I would go for seventh grade. The school district decided that students and their parents could have "freedom of choice" in choosing the school each student would attend the next fall. All schools were open to all students. No school was fully integrated. Either the junior high school was all-black, or it was predominantly white. The exception to that rule was J. A. Trice Junior High School. It was a new school that opened near the campus of predominately white Pine Bluff High School.

Perhaps the school district administrators thought that parents and students would voluntarily fully integrate the schools, but that did not happen. The courts ruled that integrating public schools was the law, but the citizens charged with enacting the law had not changed their hearts, and they were not prepared to accept the law. Folks chose to send their children wherever they wanted. Southeast Junior High School was closest to our home and all black, but I chose to attend Trice. I wanted to experience an integrated school because I was curious and felt confident in my ability to succeed there. Many of my friends chose to attend Southeast, but I wanted an opportunity to compete academically with white males, who it seemed ran everything in our community.

During the summer of 1969, Mrs. Hatcher and her husband, Gilbert, took three male classmates and me on a road trip to Texas. None of us had ever left Arkansas. Mrs. Hatcher spent time in foster care as a child, and our trip was a visit to see her siblings. We thought packing food for the journey was a neat idea. We didn't understand that racial tensions forced them to pack food for us. It was my first vacation trip. The boys and I took turns riding in the front seat between the Hatchers. We never thought about our blackness while traveling with white adults. She was our teacher, and we trusted her. Our parents trusted her, too. We were gone for a week, and when we returned later than expected, we found Jimmie waiting on the front porch with a wrinkled forehead. She was gracious, however, and thanked them for taking care of me.

5

The Trice Experience

My sixth-grade teachers recommended me for placement in advanced English and mathematics in seventh grade. I also signed up for band to learn to play the flute. The band directors were pleased when they realized I could already read music; after all, I had taken piano lessons for three years prior to seventh grade. With the exception of my English teacher, all my teachers were white. They saw that I was an amiable child, who was willing to work hard to earn A's. My regular classes had a mixture of students with varying abilities. In the two advanced classes, only a handful of black students were enrolled. I only remember a couple of other black girls in my classes and a few black boys. Not everyone had equitable access to the advanced classes. Placing students in those classes was subjective and based on teacher recommendation and grades on class work.

Seventh grade was also the year that girls could no longer wear pants to school. We had to wear skirts or dresses in grades seven through twelve. Steffy's was a children's shop in town which specialized in beautiful dresses for girls and teens. Dollee discovered the shop as a result of her work as a domestic. It seemed the well-to-do bought dresses there for their daughters, and that was where my mother and aunt bought a dress wardrobe for me. They put a couple of dresses on layaway and paid on them over time until they paid them in full. By the end of the school year, I had a lot of dresses, but at the end of the school year, the district changed the policy and said girls could wear pants to school. Throughout junior high school, although the rules were relaxed and hip-hugger jeans and bell-bottom pants were *en vogue*, I had to wear dresses to school every day. I always dressed nicely, but I did envy the girls who wore the stylish jeans, big buckle belts, and wide-lapel, colorful blouses.

The Trice experience proved to be an interesting time in my life. I made new friends with black students from the west side of Pine Bluff, and I met a variety of white students, whose families were big shots in town, who owned businesses and ran the city. That year, I also met my biological father for the first time. Up until that time, I had no clue as to who he was or what he looked like. The previous summer, after being enlightened by the neighborhood kids, who said that it took a man and a woman to make a baby, I pressed my mother about my father's identity. I had never seen him or heard his voice.

One morning, as Jimmie was dropping me off at school, she got out of the car and said, "Come on." (Usually she just dropped me off and kept driving.) She walked me over to a car and told me to get in. I wasn't sure who the man was in the front seat, but my gut let me know who he was. As I sat in the car, my mother leaned into the car window and talked to him. Her voice sounded like one of the adult characters from a Charlie Brown special. All I could hear and remember is "Wah-wah-wah-wah." I know she said something intelligible, but I was in a fog, trying to process what was happening. What was I supposed to think? How was I supposed to behave? What was I supposed to call him? Nothing seemed appropriate. Then, I asked him his name. He told me his first name, and I asked him his last name. All of that seemed strange, but at twelve years of age, I didn't know how to process the meeting or what to say, to think, or to do. I was the child in the midst of a situation that was not my making. I wasn't angry or frustrated; there was no feeling, not even numbness.

Neither of them told me who he was. I had to guess. I don't remember much of the conversation we had that morning, except when he asked about Buster. He then gave me a handful of change and told me to share it with my brother. I showed the change to a friend, who suggested we go to the nearby drugstore for candy. We left school, bought candy, and made it back to school in time for our first period class.

I don't know what my thoughts were that day about meeting him, except, it just seemed strange that I had met him for the first time in front of my new school. For the rest of that year, he showed up periodically in front of the school in his late model lime green Pontiac. Each time I talked to him for a few minutes, and he gave me a handful of change. I never knew when or if he was going to show up. He just did, and like everything else about him, his presence or his absence held little meaning for me.

Over time, I learned what a father is supposed to be and to do for his children. As far as I can remember, he never held my hand. I never sat on his lap. I never knew what made him laugh or what upset him. I don't know what he smelled like because he never hugged me. There was never an exchange of "I love you." He never knew what I liked or disliked or even that red is my favorite color. I never knew if his hands were rough or soft, and I don't ever remember having a gentle father's touch. So his presence on those mornings held little significance for me. It was nice to know I wasn't asexually reproduced, as I had imagined, but meeting him did not change anything about how I lived, grew, or learned.

After that school year, he and I never had another conversation, although occasionally, I saw him driving down the street. Just as strangely as he had appeared in my life, he had disappeared like an apparition, and I never heard from him again. Apparently, he had only felt safe coming to Trice that year because it was far enough from the east side of town where his wife and other children lived.

The next year, when I went to Southeast Junior High School on the east side, it wasn't safe for him to meet me at school because his neighborhood store was near there. I always listed him on any application as deceased, for he *was* deceased, as far as I was concerned. I knew I could never count on support from him. That's the situation whenever someone dies. You understand that their capacity to love and to support you has ended. He never had the capability of loving and caring for me. He never lived as my father. He was always dead. When he took his last breath twenty years later, I felt nothing. There was no emotion attached to knowing who he was because there was no real relationship between us.

Sister Ora called our house to announce his passing. It was as if I were supposed to care, or at least, have a thought about him. I had nothing, absolutely nothing. A few days later, I read his obituary out of curiosity and learned how old he was, his address, and the names of his other children. I felt no sense of loss or sadness, and I certainly shed no tears.

I have tried to think about the potential effect of not knowing a father in my life has had on my general well-being. Not much. I couldn't miss what I had never had. I never mentioned him to any of my friends, and guys I dated never heard me utter a word about him. I grew up feeling whole and complete because I had the caring touch and love of two adults, my mother, and my aunt. I didn't know I should have had more, so I never felt neglected or abandoned.

***

I only spent one year at Trice. I experienced the ups and downs of adjusting to junior high school work and the onset of puberty. Mrs. Worley, my geography teacher, taught us about Mao Tse Tung in China. She pronounced his name as "mayo-toose-tong." Later, I figured out the correct pronunciation of Chairman Mao's name. My seventh grade English teacher, Miss Callaway, taught us about noun clusters. I don't know who taught her about them, but none of my English teachers since that time ever mentioned them. (They are a string of nouns that often confuse readers, and which writers should avoid.) In math class that year, I struggled with ratios, finally mastering them with the help of my teacher. In band, I earned first chair flute.

Using some of the quarters, nickels, and dimes from the loose change my father had given me, I bought books when my English teacher placed her orders. I purchased paperback copies of *The Music Man, Mod Squad,* and *Cheaper by the Dozen*, and began my own home library. I cherished books, especially the feel and the smell of them. I liked turning the pages of a good book, and I spent hours reading, especially to avoid housework.

In the fall of 1970, schools in Pine Bluff integrated fully, both students and teachers. Trice became part of Pine Bluff High School, and students who had attended Trice were divided among the four junior high schools. The two all-black high schools were converted into junior high schools. Similar conversions took place all over this country as all-white school boards determined that the all-black schools did not have adequate education facilities and resources to continue as high schools for both black and white students. The schools, however, had been adequate when they housed only black students. The school principal positions at the former all-black schools were handed over to white men, and the former black high school principals were demoted to assistant principals under a white man at the high school, who had less leadership experience.

Buster and I ended up at Southeast Junior High School. Like LaWanda and Marion, we became Southeast Panthers and sang the school spirit song, "Southeast Panthers got the shoo-rah, the dooby, dobby, doo-rah."

6

Southeast Panthers Got the Shoo-rah, the Dooby, Dooby, Doo-rah!

1970 was the first full year of public school integration in Pine Bluff public schools. Full integration did not occur on its own with the full consent and cooperation of the people across America. As in communities throughout America, the courts enforced public school integration laws. The ruling of the U.S. Supreme Court in the *Brown v. Board of Education Topeka, Kansas* decision became the law of the land in 1954; however, separate but equal had remained the practice of many school districts. Pine Bluff School District complied sixteen years later.

Black and white students from different communities, both rich and poor, attended school together under court order. There were no fights or public demonstrations, either for or against busing in Pine Bluff, but we did have our share of other threats. A friend once said, "Just because the courts ruled that we must integrate our schools doesn't mean our hearts have changed." He was right.

"There's been a bomb threat. Please evacuate the buildings." Those were the words of Mr. Brooks at least once a week over the intercom at Southeast Junior High School that first year. Dutifully, we filed out of our classrooms into open areas of the campus and we waited for an all-clear signal to leave the school grounds. There was no caller ID back then to track or trace calls, so anonymous calls were made from home phones and pay telephones to schools throughout our district indicating that a bomb was set to go off at any minute. Police came with bomb-sniffing dogs. Once outside the buildings, we were eventually sent home. No visits to lockers for anything. School officials sent us home. Fortunately for us, no one was afraid, and no bomb was ever found. Folks assumed it was a prankster making a call to get out of school, or someone who opposed full integration. Initially, the local news reported those threats, but like any recurring hostile event, we became de-sensitized to the shock of those threats and accepted them as a part of our regular school day.

Southeast was within walking distance of our home. We had moved to our new house on East 19th Avenue the summer before I entered eighth grade. It was my first memory of moving, and I was thirteen years old. So, although my mother and aunt were both single parents, there was stability in our home, and we were never concerned about our address or where we would sleep each night.

We moved once, and we had the same telephone number for many years. To acquire this home, my mother and aunt pooled their resources with help from LaWanda, bought a piece of land, and built a house on it. Two economically disadvantaged black single parents building a new house was rare.

Unlike our rental house, our new home was built under Jimmie's constant gaze. She visited the site daily, sometimes more than once, and made sure that the construction was completed to her satisfaction. Although she had never built a home, she had an idea about it should be constructed. She demanded that the builders fashion everything to her satisfaction. White siding covered the exterior, paneling covered the interior walls, and tile covered the floor. A galley kitchen led to our backyard. Jimmie found loads of dirt to fill holes in the front yard. She and Buster spread dirt and planted grass seeds. When the seeds sprouted, no one walked on Jimmie's grass. Dollee grew yellow squash, tomatoes, okra, and peppers in the backyard. She also planted Cape Jasmine bushes under the front windows. We were pleased to have a nice place to call home—a place where we were proud to have friends visit us.

Southeast Junior High School was the home of the Panthers, and our school colors were orange and black. We sang *"Southeast Panthers got the shoo-rah, the dooby, dooby, doo-rah,"* at athletic events. With each verse, revelers substituted "Southeast Panthers" with a beloved staff member's name. No one really knew what the *shoo-rah* was, but it was a tune that united the Panthers in school spirit, and its rhythm provided just the right beat for dancing cheerleaders and prancing majorettes in white tasseled boots. The school's mere existence as a junior/senior high school was a source of pride for blacks on the east side of Pine Bluff. Attending Southeast was supposed to be a place of learning and joy for black students. With integration, it became less so for us.

In eighth grade, I first glimpsed the inequities within schools. I didn't know what to call it, but I knew in my spirit that things were not right for black students. Southeast had been an all-black school for students in grades seven through twelve, and now, with white teachers and white students added to the mix, the black students were put at a disadvantage in what had previously been their own learning environment. How could these white folks come to this campus and take over, acting as if they were better than the black folks who had been there all along? I had many lessons yet to learn about bias, privilege, and power in American education.

The school placed me in an advanced English and mathematics classes, as well as some of the students with whom I had attended elementary school, but who had not gone to Trice. We began the school year with about eight to ten black students in those classes. Just as happens today, I watched the white middle-class teachers teach the white middle-class students with no effort to differentiate their instructional strategies or language to meet the learning needs of the economically disadvantaged black students. For instance, we never read poems, essays, books, or articles written by people of color, so it was usually difficult for us to connect personally with the literature. Any connection would be artificial at best. In addition, tasks like conjugating verbs were foreign to all of us, but for some reason, the teachers pushed and prodded the white students in ways that they didn't do with the black students, including me. They gave their instruction, describing the content in a way that was appropriate for the white students, and we had to catch on the best way that we could.

As a result, many of the black students did not perform well. Two factors worked against us. First, the teachers held low expectations for black students and taught them with little to no expectation that they were capable of achieving at high levels. Second, some of the black students doubted their own abilities to perform at high levels with white teachers, and performed poorly, defeated in their own minds, spirits, and hearts. I didn't buy into that notion. White students, who were often not as apt as the low performing black students, were coached, supported, and encouraged by the white teachers, and allowed to stay in the classes. That did not happen for any of the struggling black students, especially those who did not make the grades to remain in the advanced classes. Equity did not exist in those days, and for many students of color and poor students, it still does not exist.

By the end of the first nine-week grading period, we began to lose black students from the advanced classes. With each subsequent grading period, we lost more black students. What hurt the entire school community was the double whammy which the black students felt as they left the advanced classes. Some of the black students, who were in the advanced classes, were also cheerleaders or athletes and were required to maintain a C average in all classes. In order to remain in an advanced class, a student had to have at least a C. Getting dismissed from an advanced class meant they had less than a C, and it therefore meant they were also dismissed from cheerleading and athletics. That left the majority of the cheer squad to the white girls, some of whom were also in the advanced classes. They were not any smarter than the black girls and black boys who were dismissed from the advanced classes. The white students received instruction in a way that met their learning and cultural needs, while the black students had not. In my childhood mind, I thought it was wrong. It was a major social and academic injustice for children of color in our community and all over this country. The black students who succeeded were those who readily adapted to the ways in which the white teachers taught. My Trice experience with white teachers the year before helped me adapt and maintain top grades.

Like a pebble thrown into a calm pond, the impact of these student dismissals from advanced classes reverberated throughout the school community. Some of the students who were dismissed from these classes were my friends, and when the dismissals happened, as a child, I did not know how talk to them about what happened. We knew it was wrong, but we did not have the language or the skill needed to appropriately process our thoughts and express our angst. Neither did our parents.

Everyone knew that racism was at play, but we didn't know what to do about it or how to articulate our disgust in a way that would have remedied the situation. The dismissals caused shame for the black students in ways that neither they nor their parents could alleviate. These dismissals sent intentional erroneous messages to all students. The white students were affirmed in their notions of superiority to black students, and the black students were confirmed in their feelings of inferiority and self-doubt in integrated settings. Neither notion was true, yet it persisted in our school and in schools throughout our community. Unfortunately, for some, those notions of inferiority and self-doubt remained with them throughout junior high school, and I suspect for some, those feelings lingered much longer.

***

Racist. Racist practices. Prejudice. Inequities. Inequalities. Discrimination. Prejudice. No one wanted to talk about or use those words. Those are the best words to describe the challenges endured by black students and their parents all over America as schools integrated. Although black students were the victims, perspectives of those situations were often reversed, and we were made to appear as the offenders as if we were unworthy of having the same opportunities for academic success. And even though we were in the same classrooms with white students, the opportunities for success were not the same, and it was often made to look like our lack of success was due to our own lack of effort, inferior ability, and race. Unfortunately, for many, the notion of unworthiness seeped into their spirits and became inhibitors of the desire for more above and beyond what they saw at Southeast and in Pine Bluff. That was not the case for me.

7

Write On!

I am. We are. They are. Verb conjugations, ugh! On the first English test on verb conjugations, I missed all the points for correctly conjugating the verb "to be." I misread the directions and thought it said to conjugate any verb. My grade on that test was not pretty, and I knew I had to ace everything else to receive an A in eighth grade advanced English. We learned to conjugate most of the irregular (*i.e.*, come, run, be, etc.) verbs that often challenge adults in speaking and writing. We also learned how to diagram sentences and how to correctly use the parts of speech. Our teacher believed that to write well, we had to first learn how to use the English language correctly. And so, we did. Little did I know that I would see verb conjugations again in French class.

Young adult literature was also a part of our curriculum. We filled our brains with ideas from texts before we wrote. We read books as a class which had nothing to do with who I was becoming; I didn't identify with the characters. We read about young white boys and their American adventures and pursuits -- stories like *Johnny Tremain*, *Huckleberry Finn*, *Old Yeller* and *The Red Badge of Courage* with which our teacher was most familiar. It was as if the stories of young black boys and girls didn't matter. I wondered why we never read books that had black male or black female protagonists. Weren't their stories equally as powerful, engaging, and important? William Armstrong's *Sounder* would have been the perfect partner novel for *Old Yeller*. I did not see myself in the curriculum, but I persevered.

We also read books on our own and wrote book reports. Each report had to be a short summary of each book---no retelling and no specific details. The reports were handwritten in small boxes about an eighth of the size of a letter-sized sheet of paper. I questioned why our teacher wanted us to write so little. I understood later the importance of writing succinctly. It was Shakespeare who wrote, "Since brevity is the soul of wit..., I will be brief." We had to demonstrate our writing proficiency clearly in as few words as possible.

I had the same teacher for ninth grade advanced English with the same students from my eighth grade class. Our teacher continued her style of teaching, and I worked even harder to get A's. After all, ninth grade courses counted towards high school graduation. I read Maya Angelou's *I Know Why the Caged Bird Sings* one term. Although she was black and from Stamps, Arkansas, I struggled to make a meaningful connection to the pain in her life. Particularly disturbing to me was her description of her rape. That scene stirred fears in me that caused nightmares and made writing my report a challenge. There was so much to tell, and so little space in which to tell it. I managed to eke out a respectable summary to maintain my "A."

Our teacher invited us to polish a piece of writing to submit for consideration of publication. Students in the advanced class accepted the invitation and prepared a piece. To our surprise as impressionable teens, everyone's work was accepted and published in a book of student essays. The catch that we had to order a copy of the book if we wanted to see our work in print. The book came in a soft pink cover. It was my first publication.

8

Peaceful Protest

Scientists say it's time for some birds to leave the nest when the bird gets too big for it. The fledglings must figure out a new place to live. They get out and try their own wings and see if they can live, find food, and make it on their own. I guess that is what happened to me in ninth grade. Integration was still fresh, and while the children handled it with ease, that was not always the case with the adults, especially the black adults. It was time for me to go. I didn't know where I would go, but I just knew I needed something different.

In eighth grade, I held first chair flute most of the year with a hiccup here and there, losing occasionally to a ninth grade girl. I wasn't really challenged until the next year when the up and coming white flute players wanted my seat. Cynthia and Ann were surprisingly good flautists, and it was no secret that each believed she deserved to be first chair. They knew how to use vibrato when they played, and although I had not completely mastered that skill yet, I had spent two weeks at a summer band camp at the University of Arkansas and learned additional techniques to enhance my performance.

Each week, our black band director allowed challenges for a chair. In a challenge, each flautist played the same piece for him. He didn't use an objective rubric for judging performances. Subjectively, the director decided on the best player. That person won the challenge. I beat Cynthia and Ann for several weeks. One week after a not-so-clear winning competition, the director declared that we had tied in our performances. Cynthia had been gunning for my position. Usually, in a tie, the person maintained her seat, but not this time. The band director gave my seat to Cynthia. Of course, she was happy, and I was not happy. Cynthia finally had first chair.

My friends who listened to our competition sided with me. Leaving the band room that day, I fumed with anger. I was robbed and would have to fight to regain first chair. And although I would no longer be there, I still had to play the first flute part with Cynthia and Ann. That was not right. If they were that good, they should have been able to carry the first flute part by themselves.

That night, Jimmie became quite angry when I told her what had happened. I explained the entire situation to her and told her just how unfair the band director had been. My mother was still paying for piano and flute lessons, and she expected a top-notch performance from me in anything related to music.

The next day, Jimmie went to the school. She asked to meet with the band director. School personnel never liked to see my mother coming to the school. They knew her presence there only meant trouble for them (*i.e.*, greater accountability for them and their decisions and behaviors).

It was an indication that school officials had made some sort of blunder, which she uncovered. This visit was no exception.

The band director shared the results of our challenge performance and indicated that there was a tie. Jimmie questioned him about his past practice of retaining the seat in the event of a tie. He indicated that was, indeed, his practice, but now, he needed to have some white students in first chair in band. Why did he say that? His statement brought down the true wrath of Jimmie Pendleton. She told him about his fear and how disappointed she was in his cowardice as a teacher and black leader in the school and the community. (My mother never understood why educated black folks would be afraid of anything or of anyone. She did not have a high school diploma, and yet, she feared nothing.) Jimmie always spoke her mind, and she didn't care who disliked what she said. She never backed down. She told him how unfair that was to me as a member of the band who worked hard for everything. Jimmie ended the conference by telling him that if he couldn't fix the situation, I would move to last chair and play the fourth flute part. And so, it was. We had a band concert that week. I sat in last chair and the fourth part was the strongest on the night of our performance. While it hurt my feelings to be in last chair when I knew I was capable of so much more, I learned to like the other flute players. It was a whole lot more relaxing in last chair, and I had a new opportunity just to enjoy band and play the music. I understood the importance and power of peaceful protest when facing an injustice, and that comforted me.

I still earned A's in English, and I still made the honor roll every grading period. The only B on my report card was in Algebra I. I thoroughly enjoyed my teacher because she was kind and she patiently offered additional support to all her students, no matter their color or economic status. She was a nice white lady.

That year, I began to feel myself change as a human being. For the two years I'd had my menstrual cycle, I suffered with painful cramps every month with no relief until after the third day. If I ate anything hot or cold or sweet or salty, it made the cramps worse. I had at least three days of misery each month. The cramps got so bad one day in Algebra, I passed out at my desk. I put my head down for a minute and woke up a few minutes later, disoriented. The teacher promptly sent me to the office to go home. She knew something was wrong because I had never fallen asleep or been anything less than attentive in her class.

***

Although the band marched on the field only once during football season, we practiced daily for two weeks before school started. We also practiced each morning on the wet football field, during first period of the fall semester. I dreaded feeling the wetness on my feet. We tracked dirt, mud, and grass back into the school building. No one had the presence of mind to provide space for cleaning our shoes, and we weren't allowed to get paper towels from the bathroom to clean them. That would have meant a hall pass for each of us, and no one was going to ask for that.

9

First Amendment Consequences

Merrill Junior Senior High School was the first and largest all-black high school in Pine Bluff. Southeast Junior Senior High School was built years after Merrill, and black students in grades seven through twelve from the east side of Pine Bluff attended school there. Folks came from as far as Packing Town, Moscow, and Vaster (small southeastern communities) to attend Southeast. It was there that black students developed friendships that lasted for decades.

The only two black high schools in Pine Bluff public schools, Merrill and Southeast, were cross town rivals, and even after the high schools were no longer in existence, the junior high schools continued the rivalry. The Southeast vs. Merrill football game had the largest attendance, and the tension was always high. The night of that game in ninth grade was no different.

When Southeast lost the football game, we were crushed that we had lost the game in our last year of junior high. The football players, who were our friends, were sorely disappointed and held their heads down as we left the stadium. As band members, however, we thought we had a right to openly display our disappointment with the team's performance.

I started the barrage of negative comments with, "Y'all ought to be shame of yourselves, losing to Merrill like that." That wasn't enough.

I continued, "And you're *sorry*, too." At that point, my fellow band members Ruby, Tammy, and Vicky joined in making comments that would be later viewed as harassment. We wanted them to know how we felt, and we believed that we had a right to express our thoughts. Not everyone agreed with that sentiment. We had freedom of speech, but we were not aware of the consequences that accompanied exercising our rights.

The football coach was not happy with his team's performance, and he was even more displeased with the comments from us band members. Coach Jones reported our behavior to Mr. Carlton, our band director, who promptly reported it to the assistant principal, Mr. Larson, who was not a fan of me or my mother. It was a strange situation because Mr. Larson's father was a member of our church, and he adored me. His father called me his "Little Pianist," partly because of my size, and partly because of my age. Whenever he needed music played, he would ask me to come to the piano and play for him. In any case, Mr. Larson did not like my mother's boldness in speech. In those days, women were not supposed to have an opinion, let alone have a voice and the courage to express it. Jimmie had both.

The day after the football game, I and my band companions, who had voiced our opinions, were summoned via intercom to the office. Upon hearing my name called, I had to swallow hard to keep my heart from jumping out of my chest and out of my mouth. Enough had already come out of there the previous night. I knew that I was in trouble, and I had no idea how Jimmie would respond.

I waited nervously for my turn to talk to the assistant principal. What I didn't know was that my mother had already been called and asked to come to the school. I watched as my friends left the office with their parents, not exactly sure of anyone's fate was. My bony knees knocked together. I was an A student. I had never been in trouble at school, and ninth grade didn't seem like the time to start. As usual at lunch that day, I had only eaten half of what was on my tray, so my stomach churned making unusually loud noises. I could feel and hear the juices gurgling.

When Jimmie arrived, she gave me that look…the look that meant "go to hell" for some folk, but it meant "just wait until you get home" for me. My mother knew I was a talker, but she also knew that I had the good sense to know when to cut things off so she would not have to leave her hourly wage job and come to the school over foolishness. I had pushed the conversation too far, and here I was in the principal's office for misbehaving. Jimmie sat down beside me, and we waited for Mr. Larson to call us into his office. Jimmie didn't like Mr. Larson, and he didn't care for her, either. I knew up front that it was going to be a difficult meeting.

Once we settled in his office, Mr. Larson relayed the events of the night before. He said, "Your daughter is accused of harassing football players after the game last night. Mr. Carlton, the band director, and the football coach complained that Veda and some other girls had a lot to say to the players after we lost to Merrill. Now, we can't have that."

"Exactly what did Veda say?" Jimmie asked.

"I don't know because I wasn't there," he replied.

"So you brought us in here, and you don't know what she said. And you weren't a witness to any of it?" my mother asked.

"Ah, yes," he answered slowly.

"Well, how do you know if she did what they are saying she did?"

"I am taking their word for it. They are the teachers."

"I don't give a shit who they are. Did they hear her say anything?" She pressed and gave him her notorious *"go to hell"* look.

"I think the football coach heard them, and he reported it to Mr. Carlton. And the players also said it happened," he continued.

"Well, Veda, what happened?" Mr. Larson inquired of me.

Slowly, I thought about what my response should be. I knew, above all, I had to tell the truth. Jimmie detested liars, so no matter what, honesty was best. My life would be much worse if I lied. I mulled my words over in my head wondering how best to craft a response. I measured my thoughts and my words carefully. I could not remember the last time I had lied to Jimmie. Whenever it happened, her response must have been traumatic because I blocked it out. Now was not the time to experience her wrath again. I didn't want to get in trouble at school, but my fear of Jimmie was worse than anything the school could do.

"I did say some things to the football players. I told them that they could have done better and that they should be ashamed of themselves. That's all I said. The other girls said a lot of other stuff, but I got on the bus," I stated.

"I told you, you didn't need to ride the bus," Jimmie said.

"I know," I said, holding my head down.

"So, based on Veda's own confession and the reports from the teachers, I think a suspension is in order," Mr. Larson said.

"Hold up! Wait just a damn minute! You mean you are going to suspend her based on hearsay from the teachers? Veda has never been in this office for so much as a tardy slip, and you think a suspension is in order?"

Her response surprised me, and there was so much thunder in her voice, even I shook. I knew she was getting hotter by the minute. She didn't believe that my offense warranted such a consequence. Mr. Larson knew that he was not right, but he also knew that he held the power. And despite his power, he knew that if Jimmie got really mad, she would rain down fire on him and on everyone else in the office. He decided to compromise.

"Veda's suspension will be for the rest of the school day. That's three class periods," he said. "That way, she won't miss a whole day of school."

Without speaking a word, Jimmie gave him that look again, and he knew what she meant. He knew that he had just dodged the bullet, one that would have ricocheted and found itself lodged in his throat and in the throats of the principal, the counselor and the school secretary who overheard the conversation. Everyone would have been choked up had Jimmie blown her top. She was no joke and not one to be reckoned with when she was angry. At home, my brother and I were afraid of her, and we thought everyone else was afraid of her, too. Mr. Larson was no exception.

We left the office peacefully. My thoughts immediately went to the classes I would miss that day. I never wanted to miss Algebra because learning Algebra was like learning French. I needed to practice it every single day. Missing Civics and Mr. Neal's science class would not make that much of a difference. After all, Mr. Neal never taught. He just had us complete self-selected science modules each week. Once we completed a module, we took a test on the material. We spent the rest of our time in his class playing Battleship on hand-drawn grids on blue-lined notebook paper or playing football with triangular-shaped paper footballs across our desks. In Civics, Mrs. Cromer would allow me to make up the work. She liked me as much as any white teacher could like a black student in newly integrated schools.

"That damn Mr. Carlton. He did this. He's been mad at me since the problem with first chair. He wanted to get back at me. But that's okay. He will get his." Jimmie was furious.

She didn't fuss at me. She already knew about my mouth and how much I talked, both in school and at home. There were times at home when she couldn't stand my voice and the way I sassed her. When arguing, we both wanted the last word. She usually got it. Sometimes, I got the back of her hand across my lips.

To my surprise, there was no additional punishment at home. It's not like there were privileges to be taken from me. I did not have a bicycle to ride after school. I did not receive telephone calls on school nights (my choice). There were no video games to play, and we only had one television, which everyone watched together. Cooking was already my after school responsibility. Buster did the dishes and cleaned the floor. The only other option was to whoop my behind, and she chose not to do that. She knew that I was already disappointed because I would not have perfect attendance like I had the previous year. I was also frustrated that I had misbehaved in a way that brought my mother to school and brought me shame. Lastly, I was saddened by how I had hurt my friend. He had done his best that night. It just wasn't supposed to be a win for us. My spirit ached.

We drove home, and I started dinner.

***

I have thought of that day and how exercising my *First Amendment* rights got me in hot water unnecessarily. I knew I didn't need to say all I had said, and I stopped talking before my friends did. I thought about how I hurt my friend who was on the football team, but he and I never spoke of that night or the events that followed.

This event, like other mistakes in my life, serves as a constant reminder of the frailty of the human spirit and the undeveloped minds of humans under the age of twenty-five. I also learned about the damaging power inherent in unkind words. It would be a few more years before I would learn and take heed to the scripture about life and death being in the power of the tongue.

10

Risk Tolerance

In the midst of all of this confusion about band and a suspension, I had the wherewithal to consider applying to a preparatory (prep) school. Marion had gone to Phillips Exeter Academy in New Hampshire six years prior, and it was a wonderful academic and personal experience for him. He grew into a more thoughtful and reflective person who took the time to teach Buster and me some of what he learned there. His stories made me curious about other learning opportunities for me.

I knew I needed more than what Pine Bluff schools and my community had to offer me. I craved learning what was within the covers of books, and it was through reading that I was able to quench that thirst. Even more enjoyable to me was discussing what I read with others, but there was no place to do that at home or at school. Cooperative learning or seminars like the Harkness method were not on the radars of teachers in our community. Jimmie and Dollee were busy trying to survive as a low-wage laundry worker and a domestic, so intellectually stimulating conversations about books were not a priority. We talked about local and national news at home while we watched Walter Cronkite each evening, and we were encouraged to think critically about politics, religion, and the world. "Think for yourself" was a clear and ever-present mantra in our home.

At school, the teachers didn't seem to know what to do with me. The black teachers appeared to have lost their way in knowing how to best meet the needs of black students. Although they had previously taught only black students, they did not want to appear to favor black students by differentiating the lessons or messages of support, so they remained neutral. They did nothing. Their fear and neutrality did not help their black students.

White teachers made sure we earned every point we received in their classes, especially in the advanced classes. After years of teaching all white students, they were still grappling with the integration of bodies in the classroom. I wanted to grow and to develop as a student, uninhibited by the pressures of folks who did not want to see me thrive or who were afraid to help me. I worked hard as a student to get good grades, and I did not shy away from talking about my academic performance with other students and teachers. I knew that the situations at Southeast had begun to make my life uncomfortable.

Marion showed me the ropes for applying to the A Better Chance (ABC) program in Boston. He was an ABC student while attending Exeter. ABC, a nonprofit organization, has known for decades the value inherent in providing economically disadvantaged students with access and opportunity to educations at high performing public high schools and preparatory schools. ABC's founders understood that while talent is equally distributed in humanity, opportunities are not. So, in 1968, they set out to provide increased academic opportunities for talented youth beyond what their local communities offered.

ABC seeks to recruit highly skilled and academically motivated students who are experiencing poverty to become a part of their program and to enroll in preparatory schools all over America. A student must have top grades and show academic promise for consideration. In the 1970's, the student also had to be willing to leave home. I was willing, even though I had no idea where I would go to school. My risk tolerance was high because I wanted to grow as a learner. I was willing to take a tremendous chance to go to a place I had never seen, live with people I had never met, and learn things I had never imagined. To make the decision to apply, then go at age fifteen took a lot of courage, as I faced the unknown and my fears.

For Marion, the ABC experience was what he needed to develop as a young black man. He was challenged to learn at higher levels, and I am sure he observed the actions and lives of those students who were more affluent than he was. He knew, without a doubt, attending Exeter was a life-altering experience for him, and he wanted to see other folks have similar academic experiences. He talked to as many young people as he could and told us about his experience. In the end, he recruited several others to attend prep school, including me. I had no clue what I was *really* doing, but I was confident he would mentor me.

In addition to recruiting others for ABC, Marion carried himself as the model student for us *after* he went to prep school. I was curious about what he did and learned at Exeter. When he came home, he usually wore an outfit that expressed the radicalism of teens and young adults of that era. One year, he came home sporting an afro and wearing a colorful dashiki. He also donned the attire of the Black

Power movement and told us the significance of black folks wearing red (the blood shed by blacks in America), black (black people everywhere), and green (the motherland of Africa). Another year, he came home wearing a wide-lapelled tweed suit with baggy, cuffed pants and a wide-brimmed hat. The most creative outfit he wore home was a navy blue, maxi-length, wool coat and the hat. He carried a Gibson guitar case. Unbeknownst to us, he was taking guitar lessons, and he looked so different that we almost didn't recognize him as he stood out front at the airport waiting for us. At first glance, he looked like a mobster.

11

Mentor-Mentee

It was 1971. The Civil Rights Movement ushered in a wave of black pride in America. The Black Panther Party was powerful, and the Nation of Islam was making positive differences in inner-city communities. My only understanding of any of the issues came through the national news reports which were biased against any black empowerment effort. Folks in Pine Bluff just were not talking to fifteen-year-olds about activities perceived as radical black power. Marion, on the other hand, knew I needed to know what was happening, even if I wasn't involved in the activities.

Marion exposed me to the literature he had read. He brought me books like *Manchild in the Promised Land* by Claude Brown, *Soul on Ice* by Eldridge Cleaver, and *The Autobiography of Malcolm X as told to Alex Haley*. He encouraged me to read those books, as well as the poetry of Amiri Baraka and listen to the music of Nina Simone. As a teen, my favorite songs were "Young, Gifted and Black," and "Mississippi Goddamn." Marion believed I could handle such material and the music lyrics. While I could read all the words on the pages, I still needed the help of a more sophisticated reader to help me understand what these talented black men and women wrote and how their writings applied to me as a young black girl coming from the recently desegregated South. Their awakening and awareness in the inner cities were so different from my protected experiences in Pine Bluff. I knew nothing about their worlds, but I did understand the poverty and racism prevalent in many American communities, both northern and southern and urban and rural.

I hand wrote my letter of inquiry to ABC. They responded by sending me an application with financial forms and teacher recommendation forms. Confident in my ability to complete the application, I sat down and began reviewing the packet of information. I knew I would have questions about the application, so I held them until Marion made his weekly phone call home. By then, he was a graduating senior at Princeton University.

"Hello, Brother, I got my ABC application. Can you help me with it?" I inquired.

"Sure," he said confidently.

"Okay. It says here that I need to get recommendations from two of my teachers, an English teacher and a math teacher. Right now, I have a B in Algebra I, but last year I had an A in advanced math. Which teacher should I ask for the recommendation?"

"Ask the current math teacher. She can speak to your effort and progress this year."

"Okay, I can do that. I know I will have to ask my current English teacher because she was also my English teacher last year. I just hope she gives me a good recommendation."

"What else could she say?" he asked.

"I don't know. I think she likes me okay, but you never know."

"Just give it to her anyway. You don't have much of a choice."

"What about the essays? I have to write two of those. What should I do?"

"Well, first you want to contact somebody like Ms. Thomas or Mr. Stigger and see if they will have time to help you write the essay. If they agree, then you must take a draft of the essay with you. That means you must write something before you go to see them. You understand?

"Yes. How should I write it?

"Just use some scratch paper and let them look over it. They will help you make changes for a final draft."

"All right. I can do that, too. I think I can handle the rest of the application. Jimmie will have to fill out the financial aid papers. The application is due before Christmas."

"Get it in on time!"

"Oh, and I also have to take a test. The SSAT."

"Yes, you can take it at Central High School in Little Rock. Ask ABC and the testing company for fee waivers so you don't have to pay to take the test or the application fee."

"Okay. I will do that. Do you think they will do it?"

"Of course they will."

"All right. I'll practice writing the answers for the application on notebook paper before I write them on the form, just in case I make a mistake. And I'll take the recommendation forms to school and ask my teachers. My counselor will have to fill out a form with my grades on it. I'll take that one, too."

"Good idea. Y'all call me if you have more questions."

"Okay. Bye."

My third-grade teacher, Mrs. Lee, taught us how to complete applications and answer sheets for standardized tests. She said we would need to know how to do that for the rest of our lives. I practiced using capital letters on the identification form for our test. Mrs. Lee bragged about how neatly I completed my form. Her compliments gave me confidence when completing any application.

That night, I wrote my responses on notebook paper. I came to the questions about parents' names. I quickly wrote my mother's name and planned in my head to leave the place for my father's name blank. I knew I would complete the application with ease. Dollee called Mr. Stigger to see if he would help me. He said yes.

It wasn't until November that I took the Secondary School Admission Test (SSAT). Jimmie drove me to Little Rock Central High School. The forty-two-mile trek on Highway 65 North was easy, but we were not sure where to go once we got into the city. Jimmie was a fairly new driver, and Dollee did not drive at all. In fact, Marion bought the first family car when he was in college and left the vehicle with us. Up until that time, we walked nearly everywhere we went or got a ride on long distance trips from neighbors. On rainy Sunday mornings, we crowded in Mrs. Robinson's car for a ride to church. Now, we had a car. Before that Saturday morning, trips to Little Rock had mostly been to the airport to drop off or pick up Marion or LaWanda returning home for visits.

The airport exit was at Roosevelt Road, and all we had to do was turn right and follow that road to the airport. Getting to Central High School was a little more complicated. We got directions that morning from an attendant at an Exxon filling station.

I read a novel all the way to Central. I had no clue as to what might be on the test or the level of difficulty. I remembered Mrs. Lee also told me that I was a good test taker. She said I was, so I believed what she said. I knew in my heart I would test well. I believed that standardized tests were just opportunities for me to show the testing company just how much I knew, and I vowed to do my best.

Little Rock Central High School is a gigantic facility with lavish architecture and at least five viewable stories and a basement. It was evident that the builders did not have black students in mind when they built it. No black schools were built to equal the structure. This was a place for Little Rock's white students, and before full integration and the *Brown Decision*, they had planned to keep it that way. The front of the building was a familiar sight since it had been on the news and on the covers of magazines that featured stories about the Little Rock Nine. The sunlight that morning hit the blonde brick building just right, and it seemed as if the white letters shone proudly proclaiming a place where I could enter the front door.

Jimmie dropped me off, and Dollee walked me up the steps and into the building to make sure that I was in the right place. A test proctor guided me to the registration table where I signed in. Another proctor directed me to my seat. They seated us in every other desk. I was the only black student in the room. That should have been a sign of things to come. If I was the only black student in this room, what would the student population at a prep school look like?

The ABC application asked students if they had a specific school in mind they might like to attend. I thought I would like to attend Phillips Academy or Northfield Mt. Herman School, so I penned those names on my application. Marion told me about both schools, and I had written for information and applications from them. I never realized until much later how valuable Marion's insight and experiences were for me. He mentored me through every step.

***

Mr. Stigger taught English at Pine Bluff High School. He was one of Marion's teachers at Southeast when it was a segregated junior/senior high school. A heavyset black man, he always smiled and asked how we were doing. A black male high school English teacher was rare, and he had mastered the English language which made him an outstanding writing coach. He arrived at our home one evening after school. I showed him the essay questions and my attempts at drafting responses.

"So, what you have here is pretty good, but I'm not sure you have clarified some points in your essay. For instance, you have talked about why you want to go to prep school, but you have not talked about how attending prep school will help you grow as a student," he said.

I thought I was clear about my *why* for wanting to go to prep school, but I had not. I thought about my desire to leave Pine Bluff and Southeast and not attend Pine Bluff High School. That didn't seem like the right reason. I thought about wanting to leave home, but that didn't sound right, either.

"Do you think I should talk more about what attending prep school will do for me and how going to a school like that will better prepare me for college?"

"Now you're thinking! Tell me your ideas and why you really want to go to prep school."

"Well, it was good for Marion."

"But that's not a good reason for you."

"I really want to learn more. I just know I need something different from Pine Bluff High."

"Okay. So, let's talk a little about some of the things you think you will learn while you are there," he said.

"Well, I think I will learn more French. I will probably become a better writer, and maybe I can participate in a sport."

"Great! How do you think a school like that might help you as a person?"

"I'm not so sure about that right now. I am just eager to see what it's like. I know it might be hard at first, but I think I will be able to handle it."

"Let's write your essay about what you think you will learn while you are there and how you think you will grow. Write another draft, and we'll go over it."

While I re-wrote my essay, Mr. Stigger chatted with Dollee. They talked about Pine Bluff schools and what was happening with the teachers. I overheard him say that many of the black teachers were afraid of losing their jobs and were afraid to speak their minds. He didn't really explain why the black educators were afraid, but he did talk about examples of blatant racial discrimination at the schools. About that time, in walked Jimmie.

"…then, them scared n------ don't deserve to have those jobs. Give them to someone who will talk. I won't ever understand why an educated black person will not stand up for what he believes and talk. That makes me sick," she said. And with that, she headed to the back of the house.

I finished writing my essay that night on notebook paper and decided to write it on the application the next day. The second essay was a little less daunting, and I was able to complete it by myself.

I took the recommendation forms to my math and English teachers for them to complete. Before taking the forms to them, we trekked uptown to the post office, bought the five cent postage stamps, and went to Spilyard's Drug Store to get long envelopes. I supplied my teachers with addressed and stamped envelopes.

With the application completed and the testing behind me, all I had to do was wait.

12

My Journey Begins

The letter came in a cream-colored envelope. As I tore it open, excitement filled my entire body. I expected a letter from ABC, but the return address said The Ethel Walker School (Walker's) on Bushy Hill Road in Simsbury, Connecticut. I thought, "What's an Ethel Walker?" Curiously, I read the letter not knowing what to expect. It was a letter of acceptance which offered me everything I would need *financially* to attend school at Walker's. There, in black and white, was an offer for a full scholarship, which included tuition, room and board, all school books and materials, transportation costs, and a five dollar weekly allowance. It also included plane tickets to and from school three times a year and school uniforms. They even noted there would be housekeeping services to clean our rooms and a laundry service. All I had to do was sign the letter accepting their offer and return it. That seemed unreal, but I knew there was no money in our family to send me to a place like Walker's.

I showed the letter to Jimmie and Dollee. Both congratulated me and asked what I was thinking. My initial reaction was, *"It's not Andover or Northfield."* I wanted to wait and see if I would get a similar offer from them. Before I knew it, the adage about birds came out of Jimmie's mouth, "A bird in the hand is worth two in the bush."

"I know. I know," I said. "Do you think I will hear from those schools?"

"Who knows? But you have one choice already. You're going," Jimmie said.

"Can I just wait and talk to Brother first?" I pleaded.

"Yes, but he's not making any decisions for you."

That night, I told Buster about the letter and what it said. I told him I really wanted to go to prep school, but Ethel Walker wasn't where I wanted to go. On Sunday, Marion called for his weekly check-in. He was elated when I shared the news from Ethel Walker with him.

"Do you think I will hear from the other schools?" I asked.

"Probably not. ABC only does one school at a time," he said.

"They identify schools they think will be a best fit for each student, then, that is where they send your information."

"You mean, even though I put down two schools on my application, it doesn't matter?"

"Right. They try to match the student to the school where they think you will do your best. It's okay. Ethel Walker must be a good school."

"It's all girls. How will that work?

"That's not a problem. Remember, Exeter was all boys when I was there. The school will have dances and bring the boys over from the boys' schools. You will meet boys who are going to the same kind of school as you, so don't worry."

"What do you think I should do?

"If they are giving you all that you've said they are, then you should go there without a doubt."

"Okay, I guess I can work with that."

"And by the way, you should take your letter to *The Pine Bluff Commercial* so that they can do an article about you and your scholarship."

"Do you think they will put it in the paper?"

"Yes, and they will take your picture to go with it, too."

The story ran in the March 16, 1972 issue of *The Pine Bluff Commercial*. The article stated that I was going to a "college." That was all it took for my friends and teachers to assume that I was going to college at the age of fifteen. For the next few weeks, someone asked me about going to college every day, and I explained each time what prep school is and that it gets you ready for college. My explanation did not matter. They believed what they wanted to believe, so to them, I was headed off to college. After all, no one questioned what the newspaper printed. *The Pine Bluff Commercial* had to be right. My scholarship news became a source of pride for those who knew me and for our community.

My church family congratulated me and even asked me to stand in church service and be recognized for having won the scholarship. Our black Baptist church was progressive, and everyone promoted education as a means to change our lives. My accomplishment was a celebratory event for our congregation.

Winning the scholarship to Ethel Walker did nothing for my life at Southeast with my white teachers and administrators. A tradition at the junior high schools in Pine

Bluff was to recognize the girl and boy with the highest grade point average in ninth grade with the Danforth Award at the end of the year awards assembly. Everyone at school knew about my accomplishments and my grades. The expectation was that I would be the girl to receive the award. That was not so. They changed the rules without notification or warning to parents and students. The counselor and the principals decided that year to give the award to three white boys—a set of twins and one other boy. There was no award given to a girl at all. Had they given an award to a girl, it would have been me, and with a newly integrated school, they just could not stomach that. I can imagine them justifying not giving it to me by saying I was not going to high school there, so it did not matter.

Yes, this hurt my feelings. As I walked back to my afternoon class after the awards assembly, I met the school librarian, Mrs. Broughton.

"Veda, I am so glad you are leaving Pine Bluff. They robbed you. You know that was your award. Yes, they robbed you," she said.

"I know, Mrs. Broughton, but what can I do?"

"Probably not much, but they were wrong for doing that."

"It's okay. I won't be here next year. I will go on someplace else."

That night I wanted to cry, but I didn't. Tears had often been my go-to coping mechanism, especially in difficult times and with the emotions I had with my menstrual cycle. My hopes had been so high earlier that day with the expectation that I would receive that award. No one had ever indicated that I would or wouldn't, but like the librarian and possibly some others, I knew I had the top grades for a girl. I had learned another lesson about inequities in public school. It was not easy, but it wasn't as painful as it could have been. My saving grace was that I was leaving behind the injustices I had come to know in Pine Bluff. I imagined that there could be inequities in other places, but I was willing to take the risk. That year, my peers voted me "the girl most likely to succeed."

***

Marion graduated from Princeton in the spring of 1972 with a political science degree and plans to attend law school. Dollee made her one and only visit to the campus for his graduation. Since the graduating class was still all male, she took Buster with her to inspire him to strive for similar goals. With the promise of going to Walker's in the fall, I stayed home with Mama and Jimmie.

13

Firsts

A Better Chance required that I attend a three-week summer program to acclimate me to prep school life as a part of my agreement to attend Walker's. My program was at Williams College, and coming from Pine Bluff, I may as well have been traveling to another planet.

It was my first flight, my first trip traveling alone, and my first time traveling that far away from home. Jimmie and Dollee said, "Read the signs, and you will be fine." They believed that with reading I could find my way.

It was a day-long journey from the Little Rock airport to Albany, NY. Jimmie and Dollee bought me a small dark gray luggage set, and I carried three weeks' worth of clothes with me. In those days, on long airplane rides of over an hour, we ate hot meals. The first leg of my flight landed in Memphis where I boarded another flight to somewhere in North Carolina. There was a layover there, then a final flight to Albany, New York.

Joe, an ABC counselor, met me at the airport. He was a cute dark-haired Italian college student with a thick dark beard and lips that looked like he puckered every time he spoke. He wore a t-shirt that displayed huge biceps. I thought, "What a hunk!" Joe picked up several ABC students at the airport and drove us to Williamstown, Massachusetts. There was only one hitch. My luggage did not arrive on my flight. As a new flight passenger, I had not thought about the possibility of not having any clothes when I got to my destination, but that was my lot that afternoon. We arrived at Williams College in time for dinner. On the way there, Joe told us we would each have a roommate.

Yana was my Puerto Rican roommate from the Bronx. I had never met a Puerto Rican before and wasn't sure what that meant. In Pine Bluff, there were black and white people, and although Jewish people owned the local newspaper, they were white in my world. There were no Latinas/Latinos in our community, so I wasn't sure what we would talk about. I slept in my underwear and put on the same clothes the next morning that I had worn all day the day before. And although my roommate knew that my luggage had not arrived, she asked me about wearing the same clothes from the day before. I just looked at her and said, "Girl, you know my luggage did not get here."

"Oh, that's right," she said.

It seemed a strange question when we had talked about my luggage the night before. My bags arrived later that afternoon. I quickly showered and changed clothes before dinner.

The Williams ABC summer program provided rigorous coursework for us six days a week. We took condensed versions of the courses that we planned to take in prep school. In addition to those courses, we also took extra-curricular activities to enrich our time there. I took my first photography class and first African dance class. While at home, if a song I liked came on KCAT, our local radio station, I danced until the end of the song. I tried to keep up with all the latest dances, and I enjoyed moving my hips and feet to the music. Before the Williams ABC Program, I had never experienced African dance and was unfamiliar with the music. My visions of African dance were images of African groups dancing on television or pictures I had seen in our encyclopedias. I was curious about African dance, but I had no idea what to expect.

My dorm counselor was the dance teacher. Like many of us and some of the other counselors, Verna was black, economically disadvantaged, and hailed from the South. She attended an all-women's college in Vermont. She pulled her hair back in a fluffy afro, and like me, she was melanin rich. Her smooth, dark, chocolate skin glistened with perspiration when she danced.

After learning some fundamentals of African dance, Verna decided to teach specific dances that we would later perform for the rest of the students in the program. There were males and females in the dance class, which meant there would be female/male couples dancing together.

Mississippi, as we called him, was from a small town in Mississippi, and he had a crush on me. We traveled about half of our trip to Albany, NY, together, and he talked the entire trip. He told me all about his life back home and what he hoped to gain from the summer experience and from going to prep school. While he had heard of young blacks going to The Piney Woods School in Mississippi, he had never heard of or known anyone to go to prep school in the North. Mississippi was going to the eleventh grade at a school in New Jersey. Unfortunately, for him, I was not interested in him. Verna was unaware of his crush on me, and in making dance partner assignments, she put the two of us together to do a fertility dance. That was more than I could handle, and after a couple of days of lackluster performances and interest on my part, she finally asked me if I wanted to dance with him. When I said no, she released me from that dance routine and partnered him with another girl.

I was relieved, but I felt as if I had probably missed an opportunity to learn something else about myself as a performer and as a young woman. It wasn't until after the performance that I understood the implications of my refusal to dance with Mississippi. He ended up performing the piece with someone else, and they performed it beautifully. Still, in my mind's eye, I was not ready emotionally to dance publicly with a male performing a fertility dance with his hands lifting my body while touching my partially exposed flesh. Our dance costumes consisted of two strips of fabric and black leotard shorts. The top, a narrow strip of brightly colored cotton fabric, looped around our necks, crisscrossed our chests, covered our breasts, and were tied in a knot in the back. My AA-cup was secure in the fabric and remained still; others jiggled with the approving eyes of teenage boys. Our rectangular skirts were flowered pieces of cloth tied at the waist. The skirt opening showed a thigh and the leotard shorts.

I knew that fertility had something to do with sex and making babies, but I was unsure of what the dance really meant. And while my dorm counselor had perceived that I was mature enough to perform such a dance, I knew I wasn't.

***

The Godfather, Part I is one of my favorite movies. Seeing it while at Williams College ignited a lot of firsts for me. I have watched that movie numerous times, and there were activities that happened in that film that speak to all sorts of vices of which I was unaware at fifteen years of age. The content of the movie isn't what makes it one of my favorites. Sure, Al Pacino was handsome, but he is not what continues to beckon me to that movie. What continues to lure me to that film is the fact that it was the first movie where I chose where I wanted to sit. At theaters in Pine Bluff, we had to sit in the balcony while the white patrons sat below. We paid our money at the front of the Saenger Theater and then walked around the corner to the outside stairs and climbed them to the balcony entrance. Making that seat choice for the first time left an indelible mark in my memory. It meant I had a freedom in Massachusetts, which, up until that time, I had been unable to claim in the South. It was a freeing feeling, pure and simple, that I will never forget. At that moment, I could be who I was and enjoy the privilege of being a citizen in this country with freedom and rights that I could exercise. That was oh, so sweet.

Fast food for my family in Pine Bluff in 1972 consisted of burgers from Rich's. Burgers were five for a dollar and that was our dinner treat on some Friday nights. Other Friday nights, we enjoyed hot dogs and homemade French fries, or fried buffalo fish and fries. With an Italian and Greek presence in Williamstown, Massachusetts, I ate pizza for the first time. The fragrant aroma of melted cheese and marinara sauce floated to my nostrils and made my mouth water in anticipation of my first bite. I quickly wiped the corners of my mouth before I drooled in front of my peers. It was cheese pizza cut into squares. I wasn't sure what to expect from the taste, but it was warm and smooth as it went down my throat. It had all the right ingredients, especially the marinara sauce. As a youngster, I would eat anything that was red, and seeing that sauce made me happy.

Another first for me that summer was the fact that I kissed a teenage boy for the first time. Yes, Mississippi liked me, but so did Herman. The difference was that I liked Herman back. Herman was from North Carolina, he was fifteen, and he was headed to a prep school in New York called Storm King. He wasn't all that cute, but he had a swagger that made him attractive. As adolescents, we needed social interactions, and the ABC program hosted a dance. About half of us hailed from small southern towns while the rest came from one of the boroughs of New York City. There were no social norms to negotiate based on geography. We were all adolescents with hormones, energy, and interest in each other.

We handled ourselves fine until the slow jams played. The closeness of our bodies in a slow dance and the perspiration from the fast songs mixed in a way that excited us. After a couple of slow jams, folks began to wander off from the party. Of course, our ruse was that we were going to the restroom, to get water, or out for some fresh air. We needed fresh air, but we didn't need fresh air with our dance partner or the one who had just excited us. No one paid much attention to our departures from the dance floor and the building. After talking to Herman for a few minutes out of sight of the adults and everyone else, Herman kissed me, and I kissed him back. I didn't exactly know what to do, so I followed his lead. It was my first real kiss.

I was nervous all night after I returned to my dorm room. I enjoyed the kiss, but I was not ready to declare openly that I liked Herman, or anyone else, for that matter. I didn't want a budding relationship to detract from my purpose for being at the summer program or for moving forward to prep school. I mulled the situation over in my head that night and decided that Herman and I could be friends, but there would be nothing beyond that for us. The next day, I told him my decision. He was not happy about it, but he accepted it, and we stayed in contact with each other after the summer program.

14

Summer Craze

I accepted Ethel Walker's offer to attend sight unseen. I had never been to the campus or seen any pictures of it. My family couldn't send me there for a weekend visit, so the ABC Program arranged for Joe to take us for a visit. Two of us in the program were going to Walker's that year, and there were several boys going to neighboring Westminster School also located in Simsbury, CT. The Walker's tour was uneventful with the admissions representative showing us around the campus. It was summer break, so few students were on campus.

The directors and many of the counselors at the ABC program were people of color. No one told me that would not be the case at Walker's. So, when Joe took us to Simsbury for the visit, I was surprised to see all white people. Liz Henry, an admissions representative, greeted us in the lobby of Beaverbrook, the multi-purpose building and dormitory. She was friendly and gracious on our tour of the school. Unfortunately, we only saw one student, a white girl, who was busy watching an afternoon soap opera in the den of the senior dorm. Karen, a rising senior, greeted us over a bowl of popcorn and went back to watching her show. She wasn't interested in talking, so we moved on to another area.

The campus was a sprawling blanket of well-manicured lush green grass with rolling hills and paved black-top paths between buildings. A few buildings, three of which were dorms, and wooded areas lined the paths. New students lived in either Smith Hall or Beaverbrook, except for new seniors, who lived in Cluett Hall, the newest building on campus. A modern building, Cluett boasted a courtyard enclosed by floor-to-ceiling glass walls. Liz assured me that I would be living in Beaverbrook with two roommates.

I wondered what it would be like sharing a room away from home with two girls I had never met. I would be sleeping in a bed by myself. Growing up, Jimmie, Buster, and I had shared a bed. When we moved into our new home, he got his own bed and bedroom that he shared with Marion. I didn't. Since I was a girl, it was acceptable for me to share a bed with Jimmie.

The Walker's chapel intrigued me. It was pristinely white with clear windows. Our windows at St. Paul Church were green and orange stained glass. There were no pictures or placards on the walls in the chapel, just bare. Like St. Paul, a pipe organ sat up front along with a piano. I wondered what music they played and what the service was like. Marion told me that at Exeter, he attended mandatory chapel daily and a church service on weekends. I asked Liz about the chapel service. She said it was a voluntary service every Sunday at 4:00 p.m. Liz also said that, occasionally, there were assemblies in the chapel, but most all-school meetings were held in the living room of Beaverbrook.

Our tour ended with a visit to the school library and performing arts center. The library had as many books as our county library in Pine Bluff, and the arts center had classrooms, a theater, and practice rooms for piano and other instruments. Even as I viewed all of this, at fifteen, I was not emotionally prepared to take in all that I saw and figure out how to use these surroundings to my advantage. I knew Walker's was something special and attending school there would be a privilege, but I wasn't sure what I was being prepared to do in life. At fifteen, that level of self-reflection evaded me. Perhaps I should have been impressed with an 800-acre campus, but I wasn't. Understanding the magnitude of that measure of land held little significance for me. I had never imagined living on one acre, so 800 acres was beyond anything I could fathom.

After seeing the campus, I had more questions. I wanted to know about the students and how many black students were at the school. What would the classes be like? What about the teachers? Would the other students be nice to me? Would I become homesick? Could I really make it at this school? What would happen if I wanted to go home? Would anyone in my family be able to visit me? Would I survive a Connecticut winter and snow? Did the dining hall food taste good? What if I got sick? Who would take care of me?

There were so many questions swirling around in my head that I could not think straight. While I kept moving forward, there was a hesitancy about trying something so drastically different and distant from everything I knew. I had voluntarily chosen to leave home at fifteen and go to a place I had never seen, and neither had anyone else in my family. In fact, before my letter of acceptance had arrived, no one in my family had ever heard of the school. I was on my own saddled with having made one of the biggest decisions of my young life. I hoped I was doing the right thing.

The ABC program ended with a ceremony and presentations of participation certificates, and we went home. Instead of Joe driving us back, Destiny, another counselor, and her boyfriend, drove us to Albany for our flights home. After three weeks away from home, everyone was glad to be leaving. It had been an enjoyable time, but I missed my family, especially Buster. We did everything together.

I returned to Pine Bluff with no real plans for the rest of the summer. Walker's sent me a package containing summer reading that included *Lord of the Flies, A Separate Peace,* and *The Old Man and the Sea.* They assured me that we would be tested on the books during the first trimester. I had never read anything like *Lord of the Flies.* Perhaps, the fact that it was so different from what I was accustomed to reading is what has helped me remember the story.

I did the summer reading as a dutiful student, but as a reader, I found it difficult to make meaningful connections without a guide to the characters and the content. Maybe, it was because I was faced with reading more about white males and their personal quests. What was I supposed to glean from their stories about their lives and struggles that would inform my own growth and development? I just could not identify with the story lines, and it took all the energy and effort that I had within me to stick to the tasks at hand. It also didn't help that Buster and all our friends were spending their summer enjoying each other's company and visiting outside the house. And every time I spent a little too much time socializing with my friends, my seventy-eight-year-old grandmother would come to the door and remind me that I needed to read.

"Beebee, have you finished your reading?" she would ask.

"No, ma'am," I would reply.

"Then, come on back in here and read," she would say. My grandmother was not a reader, and soon after I left home for Walker's, cataract surgery stole the remainder of her partial vision and rendered her blind for the rest of her natural life.

Dutifully, and without any objection, I went inside and started reading again. It was pure drudgery as I listened with one ear to the voices of Buster and our friends in the front yard while trying to focus on reading. I ear hustled their conversations a lot that summer.

As I read the books, my southern black girl brain continuously searched for places, characters, words, or actions to make connections so that I could find meaning. There were none. Traveling unescorted through these texts without a more capable teacher-reader, I was lost. It was like repeatedly conducting an Internet search and not finding any hits. I should have taken this as a sign of the readings to come.

Near the end of the summer, a letter arrived for me from a Walker's student. She introduced herself to me as my "old girl." Walker's has a tradition that matches each new girl with an old girl, that is, an incoming student with a student who has been there at least one year in a mentor/mentee pairing. My old girl was a senior, and she lived in a neighboring state. She explained that she would be there to greet me when I arrived and that she would help me become acclimated to Walker's. I was grateful that I would have a guide or mentor to help me through the first year. I did not realize the influence Jackie would have on my first year at Walker's.

***

My time at the Williams ABC program helped me understand that a new and academically rigorous world awaited me at Walker's. Nothing was going to be easy, and I was going to have to work harder than I had ever worked. While it was frightening, I knew that I could not turn back and go to Pine Bluff High School. I just couldn't do that. I had to move forward with courage and make the best of my decision even if I was terrified. What I didn't realize was that friends and family in Pine Bluff were rooting for me and waiting to see what I would do and how I would come out on the other side. They were curious and supportive. I felt the prayers of the elders in my absence from their presence.

15

Risk: The Price of Opportunity

The yellow taxi pulled up the circular driveway in front of Beaverbrook with the trunk loaded with my suitcases and a footlocker full of dresses. I remembered the red brick façade from my brief summer visit. Families were there with car trunks wide open showing boxes and suitcases full of clothing and other belongings to ensure comfort away from home. Most of the parents drove large station wagons or SUVs that were only available to those who had money in 1972. Moms and dads dressed in what prep school parent attire that were symbolic of their socio-economic status. They wore pastels and plaids, clothing that grown folks in my community would probably not be seen wearing in public. Some wore polo shirts with a little green alligator outlined in black on the left side. I soon learned that was the Izod Lacoste symbol. The women looked as if they were straight from the pages of a Talbot's catalog or Landlubber spring collection. That look also indicated country club membership I learned later.

Others sported deep greens and reds, and almost all of them wore brown shoes with white soles and white shoelaces strung through the tops of the sides. Those shoes, called topsiders, were popular. Mothers wore small, shiny, gold earrings, another status symbol, and some of the dads puffed pipes or chewed on the ends of fat cigars as they hauled boxes and suitcases into the building.

Folks were giddy with excitement about the new adventure. Parents hugged and kissed their daughters goodbye, while others tugged at luggage as they entered the building. Returning students, who had arrived earlier in the week, came out to welcome the new students. Everyone seemed cheerful and happy to be at Walker's.

I was not so sure about my degree of happiness. My arrival on campus was solitary. No family member accompanied me. It would be months before LaWanda would be able to make it over from New York for a visit, and my mother's first and only visit to the campus would be at my graduation. There just was no money for such trips.

I took a taxi from the Hartford airport with what I had imagined I would need at a boarding school. Walker's covered the taxi fare. The school sent a list of items to bring and of possessions to leave at home. All my worldly possessions, with the exception of my piano, were packed in my luggage. The school provided basic bed linen and towels. I had clothes in my bags, dress shoes, black leather boots, a pair of tennis shoes, a clock radio, toiletries that included a bottle of prescription pills for cramps, and my flute. I wore Bass Weejuns, my school shoes. I packed my black leather coat in the footlocker. I brought a bottle of Prell shampoo and Johnson's Ultra Sheen hair grease, although I did not know how I would care for and manage my hair. I got a fresh hair relaxer before my departure, and it would be December before I would return home. The relaxer straightened permanently the kinks and coils of my natural hair rendering a straightened hairdo with the ends curled and bangs. I brought almost everything I owned. None of the other students or their families paid any attention to me, and no one offered to lend a helping hand.

The taxi driver put my bags on the sidewalk outside the building and drove away. Liz from Admissions met me outside with a warm smile.

"After your visit this summer, I thought you might not come."

"I had to give it a chance, so here I am," I replied. I was happy to see a familiar face.

We took as many bags as we could on the first trip into the building. The footlocker had to wait. Inside the building was a *hullaballoo* of activity. Girls in pastel-colored dresses pranced and moved about everywhere. The hustle and bustle of the interactions of the new students and the returning students made it a joyous occasion. They all seemed excited about the onset of a new school year.

I wasn't so sure about my level of excitement. I still had reservations. I wanted to know more, but I was hesitant about the war within me. Should I be happy to be in a new place away from family and friends? Should I be grateful for this new opportunity? What risk was I taking with my learning and development? Would I be successful at this school? What would my family and friends think if I went back home? And what about the boys? How and when would I see boys? This was my first time being with all girls. I had played football and basketball with Buster and the boys in our neighborhood growing up and had only a few female friends. What would all of this mean to me as a person and as a girl coming into womanhood? Most importantly, how would I be treated as a black girl? There were no answers to any of these questions. I had to just put one foot in front of the other one and make the best of my new opportunity in this foreign land.

At a check-in table, nice white ladies and white girls greeted me with smiles, but I wasn't at the smiling stage yet. Jimmie taught me not to smile and show my teeth, unless something was funny. At that point, nothing was funny.

"Welcome to Walker's," one lady greeted me.

"Thank you," I replied.

"What is your name?"

"Veda Pendleton."

"Oh, is that the same as Doris Pendleton?"

"Yes, ma'am, but I go by Veda."

"Oh, honey, you don't have to say ma'am here."

"Yes, ma'am. Oh, I'm sorry."

"Take this packet and complete it and go to the next table."

I continued down the row, attempting to smile at each face. What troubled me the most was that there were no black or brown faces. Not one! Except for some of the faces in my school in Pine Bluff, every face in my life had been black or brown, and here there were none. *What have I done?* vibrated in my head. I had left my Christian black family, friends, and church family in Arkansas to live and go to school at a place where there were few black people. And I didn't know a soul. What was I going to be prepped to do? Would this preparation give me more of an advantage over others who did not attend prep school? What was I thinking? Did I think that an all-white environment might be better for me to learn? I don't think so. Was I trying to get away from home? No, that wasn't it either, even though Jimmie and I had fusses and arguments that she always won. Was I trying to copy what Marion had done and get my picture and name in the newspaper? None of those reasons made any real sense to me as I pondered them in my head.

Coming to Walker's was too big a risk for me to take for any flimsy reason. It had to be much more, and it had to be some purpose that would sustain me when the times got tough and I got homesick. I had to know why I was there and what such an experience would mean for me in the long run. It was both a risk and a gift, but what price was I paying to be there? I wanted an opportunity to do better and to learn more than what had been available to me up until that point. I decided that Pine Bluff had given me its best, but somewhere in my child-sized mind's eye, that was not enough. I yearned in my deepest soul to grow and to learn. I had to try for more in a different place that I hoped would provide me with greater learning opportunities. It was a major risk for a fifteen-year-old, but I was willing to take the risk *and* pay the price no matter how costly. I kept moving.

As I neared the end of the tables, a petite, young, black woman came up to me sporting a huge afro and glasses. She held out her hand and said, "Hi, I'm Jackie. Welcome to Walker's. I wrote you and told you I'm your old girl." She had a deep southern drawl. I wondered to myself if I sounded like that. After all, I was from Arkansas.

"Yes, how are you?" I replied.

"I'm fine. How was your trip?" She asked.

Not knowing what to expect, I replied, "It was fine; just long."

"Good. I'll help you get your bags to your room, then, we can go get uniforms."

We carried my suitcases up to the second floor of Beaverbrook. Beaverbrook housed the cafeteria, a dorm, classrooms, several offices, a living room for meetings, the telephone switchboard office, a smoking room, the school bookstore, and the mailroom. The painted walls displayed pastel colors, but most of them were white or a pale yellow. Tiled floors and stairs led to the dorm. Making it up the stairs with the suitcases wasn't difficult, but hefting the footlocker was another story. On the way to my room, two more black girls greeted us at the top of the stairs. Both had afros too.

Before I left home, Jimmie and I talked about my hair care. I had hair products, but I went to the beauty shop to get my hair done, so I was not accustomed to washing my hair and styling it. I didn't know what I was going to do about taking care of it. We knew the relaxer would be manageable for about six weeks, and then something would need to be done with my hair.

I greeted the other girls and admired their afros, wondering how long it would be before I, too, sported one. Afros were the "in" thing as black people in America became more cognizant of their African roots and chose to display pride in wearing African attire and hairstyles. Black men and women embraced their natural hair traits, honoring God's gift and declaring that "*Black is beautiful.*"

The two girls introduced themselves to me as Anise and Mary. They were my roommates. Anise was from Maryland, and Mary was from New Jersey. They helped Jackie and me get my bags to the room and went back to help us lug my footlocker up the stairs. They seemed like friendly girls.

Ours was the first room on the left at the top of the stairs. We were next to the school infirmary with an outside balcony, and we had our own bathroom and a walk-in closet. It was obvious Anise and Mary had already selected their beds and placed them up against the wall. The bed left for me jutted out into the center of the room. Sheets, a blanket, a brown cotton bedspread and a pillow were neatly folded and stacked on my bed. I had to make my bed. There was also a set of white towels for me to use for the week. We got one set of towels for the week. Housekeepers made our beds and changed our sheets if our space wasn't too messy.

Anise and Mary had already claimed a small desk for their stereo equipment and other possessions. Each of us had a chest of drawers with a small mirror on top. I thought I would be comfortable in that space.

Before I began unpacking my bags, Jackie told me that I had to get school uniforms to wear that night to dinner. We had to dress in a uniform for weeknight sit-down dinners. Jackie, Anise and Mary wore pastel colored uniforms. I followed Jackie to the basement of Beaverbrook, where girls were trying on and parents were buying new and used uniforms. Parents were helping their daughters find the right sizes. Walker's took care of paying for my uniforms. All I had to do was to select the uniforms that fit me. I weighed between seventy-five and eighty pounds and wore a size four in junior dresses. Many of the dresses in my trunk were still little girl sizes twelve and fourteen. I was a thin girl.

I was outfitted with used (but new to me) pastel-colored spring and fall cotton uniform dresses with Peter Pan collars, and narrow wale, dark-colored, corduroy winter uniforms. Jackie said I could wear pants under my uniforms in the winter when it snowed. I also got a couple of wool gray skirts, white blouses, and a hunter green Walker's blazer with the school crest in gold on the left pocket. They gave me a tan trench coat to wear on cold rainy days.

Every girl had to participate in a sport, no exceptions unless there was a physical disability. Jackie informed me that for sports classes, I had to wear a pale blue cotton tunic, a white blouse underneath and matching baggy bloomers with a drawstring in the waistband and elastic in the legs. The tunic came down to my knees. How could anyone play a sport in such a hideous outfit?

"So, this is a PE uniform?" I asked.

"Well, kind of. It's a tunic, something left from the good old days when Walker's first opened," Jackie responded.

"If they wore this to play sports in, I'm not so sure those were good days." We both cackled loudly.

"You will be fine in it. Anyway, most of the girls just wear the bloomers for class and practice and wear the tunic when we compete against other schools."

"Compete? With who?"

"Yes, most of us compete in one sport or another. It's just another way of keeping us involved in the school. We play other girls' schools. You'll get used to it."

"If you say so. At home, we were either in band or PE. I plan to take flute and piano lessons while I'm here, so I thought I wouldn't have to take PE."

"No, you can take flute and piano lessons, but you have to take a sports class every trimester. You can take the same one more than once, but you have to take at least one each trimester. And you have to take a dance class. Every Walker's girl takes modern dance."

"You mean in leotards and tights?"

"Yep. You've got it." She laughed.

We left the uniform room with bundles of uniforms, physical education attire, and the coat. I had become a part of the privileged poor.

***

I was 1,373 miles from home. It was too far to drive and too expensive for frequent home visits. It was another world and one so distant in many ways from what I knew. I was in a world I respected but one I would have to learn to trust.

16

The Pets

"**D**og, don't mess with Jimmie's kids" LaWanda relayed that I had said to a barking dog one day as we walked by. I was notoriously known for my fear of dogs...dogs of all sizes, shapes, and colors. It didn't matter, and that day, as a five-year-old, I thought invoking my mother's name as an authority would ward off the dog. My sister kept me from running from a dog that day.

Rags belonged to some neighbors. He was a mixed breed who was tied up in the family backyard on a chain which he frequently broke. Rags wore away the grass in the arc of yard that he walked, so on rainy days, he was a muddy mess. He lived outside in a dingy doghouse with peeling paint, and he ate from whatever dish his owners could find (*i.e.,* a hubcap, an old bowl from the kitchen, a discarded pan, etc.) at mealtime. Never was it a dog food bowl. The children in the family took care of him, but they also mistreated him. They boasted of feeding him hot sauce and hot peppers and of throwing metal-tipped, wooden, spinning tops at his feet. They said they wanted to make him mean, and they did just that. Rags was one of the many dogs that chased me as a child.

Other images in my mind about dogs came from news reports that showed white police officers using German Shepherd dogs on screaming black youth during the Civil Rights Movement. The people who were supposed to serve and protect those youth were scaring them using canine force. That was enough to traumatize any child.

For whatever reason, I have never been able to connect with the spirit of a dog, and I have developed an unhealthy fear of them. So it was an extreme shock to me when I rounded the corner to the dining hall headed to dinner my first evening at Walker's and saw four large unleashed dogs sitting outside the door of the dining hall. I froze. A blonde lab lay lazily on the tiled floor. He belonged to the PE teacher. Two other dogs, both black and white cooled themselves on the tiled floor. The fourth dog, a red long-haired Irish Setter named Sebastian, rose and barked loudly at me. He didn't move, and neither did I. I remained frozen.

My usual response to a dog barking at me had been to run away from the dog as fast as I could. At home, my neighbors always knew a dog was chasing me because I ran and screamed to the top of my lungs. Whenever a neighbor, usually an older woman, heard me screaming, she would come outside with a broom, hoe or whatever yard implement she could find and shoo away the dog. Their shooing saved my hide many a day. When I stopped running, it always seemed as if I were going to vomit my heart and the contents of my stomach. Blood rushed to my face, and what would have been red on others just made me look grayish and ashy with fright.

When Sebastian barked at me, everyone stopped and paid attention. I am sure he could feel/smell my adrenalin rush simply in seeing four unleashed dogs. Jackie, Anise and Mary tried to assure me that the dogs would not bother me. One of Sebastian's owners, the new biology teacher, came out to calm him down. When he reached his dog, I quickly walked into the dining hall shielded by the bodies of other girls who were also entering the room. Having pets, namely dogs, lying around campus and in buildings was a part of the culture at Walker's I was not prepared to accept. I didn't know how I would handle the ever-present dogs in the buildings, but I had to figure it out.

That was not the only time Sebastian barked ferociously at me. In fact, every time he saw me, he went crazy barking. I learned that his family had just moved to Connecticut from Maine and that perhaps Sebastian had never seen a black person before. I wondered to myself what difference a person's skin color would make to a dog. Could dogs be racist or prefer the skin color of one person over that of another? How could that be? Was my skin color such a contrast to that of other humans he had seen? It had to be my adrenalin that he sensed. That remained an enigma.

Jimmie told me that some dogs are kept as pets. I thought all dogs were pets, but I soon realized what she was telling me. Without using many words, she let me know that some families treat their dogs like members of the family. They treat them with respect and provide for them in the same way that other families provide for their children. Some dogs and cats live in the house, and sometimes they eat and sleep with their owners. Pet owners buy material possessions for their animals, walk their pets, and groom them. They take them to the vet and give them medicine.

What Jimmie also meant was that when animals are treated as pets, they are loved and cared for like a member of the family, unlike the dogs in our neighborhood, which were chained outside. Rags and other dogs never went inside their owner's house and were lucky if they had a doghouse and a feeding bowl. That's the difference between an animal that is kept as a pet and other mistreated and neglected animals.

All four dogs at Walker's were pets. I was able to calm my nerves enough around Barley, the blonde lab, to pet him and rub his belly. He was so mild-mannered and gentle; he hardly barked at anyone or anything. Even when other dogs barked or were lively, Barley just sat and watched or cooled himself on the tiled floor. The other two dogs, who had shiny eyes, were also harmless and never barked. Most days, they accompanied their owner, an art teacher, to class and throughout the campus buildings. I never approached them, and they never bothered me. Just Sebastian. If he was just a pet, why was he so ferocious toward me? His reactions to me never made sense to me or to his owners.

I never ran from Sebastian, but that would not be my only encounter with him and his threatening bark.

17

School Daze

Public schools have often touted and used the implementation of school uniforms as a way of leveling the playing field. Private schools have known for ages that mere outside appearance never levels the playing field of true learning, engagement, and academic outcomes; and even when students wear uniforms, it still remains evident who the *haves* and the *have nots* are.

At Walker's, everyone knew who had money and who did not have money. For the rich, it was who had old money and who had money that was relatively new. For the white girls, a last name or a parent's position (usually the father) put everyone on notice as to the power, privilege, and money that each girl had. Folks made assumptions about your status in life, academic prowess, and promise based on what your parents did. In Pine Bluff, I had no conception of what that meant in a learning environment. I had only gone to school with middle class white students for three years, but not one had the money that some of the girls at Walker's had. Yes, some Walker's parents worked in public service as ambassadors and senators, but others had come as a result of their parents' old money—money passed down through generations. They had intergenerational wealth. I was working with intergenerational survival in America. Some families sent more than one daughter to Walker's, and some of the girls also had brothers who attended boys' prep schools in the region. It was as if the families shipped their children off for the world to rear them. It was different for me. My family wanted me to have a better opportunity to make something of myself.

For the black girls, the assumption was that we were broke, smart but broke. Everyone understood that most of us were ABC students because we could not afford to pay for a school like Walker's. The cost for me to attend Walker's was about $5,000 a year, more money than Jimmie grossed yearly. Yes, she worked hard every day, sometimes at more than one job, but her wages never reflected her talent, her commitment, or her effort.

Working in dry cleaning establishments is always hard work because you never get to sit. On days when the steam iron got too hot, or a steaming presser grazed Jimmie's arm, she would come home with burns and blisters filled with fluid on her hands and/or arms. She made less than $100 a week. Dollee's wages were less, even though she cleaned someone else's house, cooked meals, did laundry, and cared for children every day. Jimmie and Dollee's compensation did not match their work ethic, abilities, or loyalty to the people and the jobs they held. That was the way of the world in which we lived in the 1960's and 1970's. Perhaps sending me to Walker's was part of their hope that my plight in life would be different from theirs.

So, when we went to class in our uniforms, everyone understood that although we were dressed similarly, the playing field was not leveled by our attire; if anything, it heightened our awareness of the differences among us. Wearing similar clothes did not make us more alike; it just made us more curious about the lives of others. Everyone still knew the real deal about social status and financial resources, evidenced in the ways the girls accessorized their uniforms, in the shoes that we wore, and in our winter outerwear. We all knew. We never talked about it, but we knew.

My first class on my first day was English. Although Walker's was on a trimester system, some classes were yearlong. Tenth grade English was one of those classes. I remember counting the wooden, one-armed desks in class on the first day, fifteen of them for twelve students. Beaverbrook classrooms were old, yet well maintained by the custodial staff. The shining hardwood floors creaked as we entered the classroom. I am left-handed, so I looked for the nearest left-handed one-armed desk. Someone was already sitting in it. I have learned that most classrooms will only have one desk, if any, to accommodate a left-handed student. In our class, there was more than one left-handed student.

Neat piles of books covered each desk along with a bookstore invoice. Mrs. Levy asked us to write our names at the top of the invoice, the titles of the books, and then sign our names acknowledging that we had received the books. This was the process for acquiring books in each class. We did not have traditional textbooks in any class, except biology, and we read literature that covered the content in our school's curriculum. I wondered if we would diagram sentences as I had done the previous two years. There was a grammar book, but I felt that learning the basics of writing would not be a part of our instruction and learning. I was right.

In each class that day, we followed the same process for getting our materials, and in each class, we received reading assignments to complete for the next class meeting. The purpose of the school was to prepare us for college, so our class schedules were set up like college schedules. There was a Monday, Wednesday, Friday schedule and a Tuesday-Thursday schedule. The Tuesday-Thursday schedule included different classes from those we had on the other three days, so there was plenty of time to get the readings and homework assignments completed.

On my second day in my English class, the teacher called on me first. Our assignment was to read the first two chapters of *The Return of the Native* by Thomas Hardy. Prior to that assignment, I the book and author were foreign to me. The night of the assignment, I read the text as I normally read assignments for school. The author's language was different from what I was accustomed to reading, so I was lost. As my eyes glossed over the pages of the text, I was confused. Unfortunately for me, I did not bother to try to re-read any of it. I just put the book down and went on to the next task. Somewhere in between, I am sure that I took a moment to reflect on home and how much I missed everybody. As I continued to process my new environs, I began to understand that I still had to do my schoolwork, focus, and make the best of my new.

That morning in English class, the teacher, Martha Levy, asked, "What happened in the first chapter of the book?" I looked down at my book, then to my uniform, and finally at my shoes. I refused to make eye contact with her. In my spirit, I knew she was going to call on me.

"Veda, can you tell us what happened in the first chapter?

Hesitatingly, I replied, "Well, no, I can't," I said looking downward. I hadn't learned yet that white people expect you to look them in the eye when talking to them. At home, looking Jimmie or my grandmother in the eye was a sign of disrespect. To Jimmie it meant I thought I was equal to her, and she always made it clear that I wasn't and would never be. So, I did not look Mrs. Levy in the eye.

"Did you do the reading?" She asked.

"Yes, I read it all! But I didn't understand most of it."

"Well, you'll want to pay awfully close attention in class today."

"Yes, ma'am."

I sat there crushed and humiliated on my second day of class at a new school. I was the only black student in that class. In fact, I was the only black student in all my classes. Who humiliates a student that early in the course? And what student continues to tolerate teacher shaming like that? At that moment, I wanted to crawl under a desk or at least out the door. Her response to me that day set the tone for some of what would happen to me for the rest of that school year and into other classes. I had never had a teacher be so curt with me. I didn't know what to make of her response. I wondered if she had ever had a black student in class. She seemed younger than my English teacher at Southeast, so I wasn't sure how to take her response. Maybe that was just a part of her personality. My classmates just stared at their books hoping they wouldn't be next. She moved on to another student.

1972 was a difficult year socially and emotionally for many Americans. As our country was continuing to mourn the losses of the Kennedy brothers and Dr. Martin Luther

King, Jr., we (black and white individuals) had not fully learned how to relate to each other in positive and meaningful ways that would serve to lift others. The Civil Rights Movement had made segregated facilities illegal, but we had not learned how to live with and love each other. That takes time, and we had not had enough time together or enough time to process and to be reflective about what the changes meant for each of us personally or collectively to make good decisions about our interactions with folks of different races. We just didn't know how to help each other become the best each person could be.

Some people acknowledged their biases and held on to them as badges of honor. Others did not even know they had biases toward other groups and did nothing to remedy them. I was at a different place, and so was Mrs. Levy. We were new to each other and to the school community, so however harsh her words were that day, I'm not sure they were said out of recognized malice. Whether they were out of ill will or not, the impact on me was the same. It was painful, and I had had my first academic shaming by a teacher in front of my new peers.

There's nothing like being a poor, southern, black girl going to a school for rich white girls and reading about unhappy rich people. I wondered how their stories were supposed to help me grow as a thinker. Just like I yearned for social connections, I also needed literary ones as well.

That year, we read a lot of different books, but I made it up in my mind that never again would I be caught in a place where I could not discuss the reading. Sometimes, it meant re-reading the text before class if time allowed. Sometimes, I dared to read the books aloud in my study carrel in study hall. I had to learn this new and different way of thinking about books, and about reading and writing.

Once I began to figure out how to think about the content in those books, I began to actually enjoy reading works such as *The Grapes of Wrath, Death Be Not Proud, Tess of the D'Urbervilles* (another Thomas Hardy novel), *Narrative of the Life of Frederick Douglass, The Member of the Wedding, The Myth of Sisyphus, Beowulf, The Canterbury Tales,* and *The Catcher in the Rye.*

It was from the Douglass narrative that I summoned the strength, insight, and courage to become a more engaged learner. After all, while still a slave, Douglass had tricked white children into teaching him how to read and write when it was unlawful for them to do so. He liberated his mind by learning to read and admitted that once he learned how to read, he was no longer fit to be a slave. His raised awareness increased my consciousness about learning in my new environment and helped me understand that, because of this experience, I would never be who I once was. I didn't know who I would become, but I knew that I would be changed forever, and hopefully, for the better.

Learning to think about books differently sometimes meant talking to a fellow classmate about the reading, someone who understood what the text said better than I did. Often that classmate was Robin, the other ABC student that year. She was a white girl from West Virginia. Like the rest of us, she was economically disadvantaged. Unlike me, Robin was often able to connect with the protagonists in the books that we read and glean more from the texts because of her connections. She thought differently, and that made a world of difference.

Robin was brilliant, and she walked with a quiet gait swinging her arms back and forth with a sense of assuredness in who she was. She had an unruly mane of blondish curls that we sometimes fussed over and even cornrowed for her. Robin always smiled, sometimes a soft hello smile and at other times, a great big glad-to-see-you smile. She once described herself as what other whites would call "white trash." I had never heard that term used regarding white people. Up until that time, my focus had been on racial epithets hurled at black people. Sure, I had heard pejorative terms used about whites in Pine Bluff, but I had never heard a white person use a term like that about herself. Robin and I became friends, and for a short stint, we were roommates. I learned from Robin that humanity comes in all forms and colors. She was kind to me, and she tolerated my naiveté about life and schooling without criticism or judgement, a rarity I appreciated greatly.

18

Homesick

Jennifer lived in our Pine Bluff neighborhood with her single mom, a teacher who moved about a bit. Jennifer's older brother left home to go to college and never returned. That was the case with many black youths of that era. We saw early on that our town had few opportunities available for black students who were gifted, talented, and progressive. It was a place of oppression and frustration for many of us; as was the case in most communities, black children were not expected to excel, and even when we did, in spite of poor treatment, racist tactics, and low expectations, we were labeled an aberration or freak. It was as if our skin color was incapable of housing God-given gifts. If we displayed giftedness, we were abnormal black students or aberrations. That notion carried with it its own burden and emotional conflict about our identity, promise, and aspirations. When we pursued excellence and performed well, our gifts and talents were not always readily acknowledged, encouraged, or appreciated. What we knew in our hearts though was that our value as learners and human beings did not decrease based on the inability of others to see our value and our worth, so we persisted.

Jennifer and I spent a lot of time playing together. We played jacks on my living room floor, and football and kickball with Buster and the boys. I liked tackle football, but she didn't. On Friday nights when we went to the high school football games, Jimmie, Buster, and I walked by and picked up Jennifer on our way to the games. Without the benefit of having a car, we walked everywhere on red gravel roads. On Sunday mornings, if Jennifer was going to Sunday school with us, we walked by her house to get her on our way to church. She sat on the back seat with us at church even if her mother came to church later. And if we left church early, which sometimes happened when the preacher said something Jimmie did not like, Jennifer went with us out the back door of the church. She was our friend. And even sometimes when Buster and I took sides against her, she always forgave us and came back to play the next day.

Lacy was my friend who was orphaned in fourth grade. Her mother died of melanoma, and Lacy came from Los Angeles to live with her uncle and aunt in Pine Bluff. I was always anxious to make new friends, and we became fast friends at church. Lacy struggled with schoolwork, and although she knew about my grades, that was never a point of contention for us. We talked about everything on the phone and on Saturday afternoon visits. She became my confidante, and I was hers. Lacy often talked about missing her mom and living in California. When she talked about her mom, it was as if she had just died the day before. Her mother's death remained fresh for a long time, and the sadness lingered, but she always smiled when we were together.

Monica was a year younger than me. Her mother was a black business owner. We became friends at church. Sometimes we sat together in church and played pencil and paper games like tic-tac-toe and connect the dots. At other times, we spent Saturday or Sunday afternoons together riding bicycles. As we got older, we (Monica, Buster, Nick, and I) pooled our quarters, rented tandem bikes, and rode those bikes all over town. At intersections where there was no vehicular traffic, we made donuts on the bikes at the intersection, circling the four corners of the spot where the streets connected. At other times we played at Monica's house with her dolls and other toys. She took piano lessons, too, and we sometimes compared what we were learning. In junior high school, she played the clarinet in band. As we grew up, we talked occasionally on the telephone about the boys that we liked. Thankfully, we never liked the same boys.

Nick Thomas, another friend whom we played with every day, lived with his mother, stepfather, and brothers. Nick was our running buddy. We played together on the back street (a dead-end gravel road beside our house), rode bikes, and threw rocks at each other. Sometimes we had rock wars or wars in which we threw pieces of old roofing shingles at each other from behind bushes and around the corners of houses. We rolled old car tires up and down the back street to see who could keep a tire rolling the longest. Sometimes we dug holes in the yard proclaiming that we were going to dig all the way to China but stopped when the dirt turned to red clay - we thought we were getting close to the devil. Monica, Jennifer, Lacy, and Nick were like kinfolk to us, and we shared and shared alike in the experiences of growing up on the east side of Pine Bluff.

Time, circumstances, and proximity placed us there together, and we became close friends.

My closest friend though was Buster. Everything that I told the girls, I told him. We talked about and teased each other about a little bit of everything. In fact, we talked to each other so much when we were awake, sometimes we talked to each other in our sleep. Jimmie overheard us in the middle of the night on more than one occasion when she ventured to the bathroom. He was my best friend and the one I missed the most when I went to Walker's. One evening, I called home and began crying because I missed him so much. When I started crying, Jimmie asked me what was wrong. I said, "I miss Buster." They put him on the phone, and he still teases me about missing him.

I was homesick. Making the adjustment to being away from home was not an easy one. I had to get used to not seeing or talking to my friends. I wrote letters to them, but rarely did anyone ever write me. I always had something new to share about my experiences at Walker's, but as I look back on what may have been the contents of those letters, I understand that what I wrote to old friends was probably so foreign to them that they did not know what to say. Perhaps they didn't have the language to express their own feelings or their reactions. I missed our talks and visits. My departure undoubtedly left a friendship void for them, which they soon filled with other friends. After all, I had seemingly abandoned them for greater opportunities.

One home connection I had was visiting my sister, LaWanda, in New York. She lived and worked on Staten Island as a hospital dietitian. She was the first in our family to graduate college. Her place became my landing spot for Thanksgiving breaks. While there, I got to know her friends and companions and learned about living in a metropolis.

City life was no joke, and New York City just seemed like a big place full of concrete and dirt. Most people lived in small apartments in huge apartment buildings. At least, that's what I saw. That was a tremendous contrast from the green grass of Pine Bluff and the suburban green living at Walker's in small town white Simsbury. While I did not make any lasting friendships in NYC, I was welcomed by my sister's friends, and that gave me some comfort.

During my years at Walker's, I hoped that the Pine Bluff friendships would remain intact and transcend time and space, and that my relationships would endure my absence through the high school years, but that was not to be. All of us spend a lifetime starring in our own movies. No one has real time to devote to be an extra in someone else's movie, especially if the movie is being directed, produced, and filmed in a distant land with a host of other unknown characters. I wish time and space had allowed for a different outcome. I always value my friendships and try to remain in touch with people who cross my paths. That's just how I am wired. I want to remain connected to other people, but that is not the same for everyone. I have learned to accept that not everyone wants to make lasting connections.

**

My fascination with remaining connected to others came from Dollee. She was the family letter writer who worked to maintain family connections. She wrote to cousins, nieces, nephews, and siblings in cities like St. Louis, Chicago, Indianapolis, and Los Angeles to keep in touch. While growing up in southeast Arkansas, it had been easy to get to know extended family members who lived in surrounding communities. The great migration of blacks moving to the North changed that for numerous black families. It was

Dollee's letter writing which let other family members know that their change in locale had not changed the nature of their relationship to our family. She kept us connected using a steno pad, envelopes, and postage stamps. Family members often replied with wallet-size photographs of their children and family updates. Buster and I always gawked at those pictures, wondering about the lives of other children in places that were foreign to us, and reveling in the thought that we had cousins our age out there whom we would someday meet.

Before I left for Walker's, Dollee promised to write me while I was away at school, and she was not short of her word. She wrote often, sometimes weekly and sometimes two or three times a month. Occasionally, she would change it up and write the letter to me from Mama. Sometimes she slipped a few dollars in with the letter. In her letters, she always reminded me that she loved me and encouraged me to always pray, to work hard and to go to church, even if the church service was different from St. Paul. Her gentle reminders kept me afloat.

Dollee's letters also kept me abreast of family and community news from Pine Bluff. She told me about Mama losing her sight with her cataract surgery. It was supposed to improve her sight, but it didn't. She also let me know when there were deaths. One letter my second trimester at Walker's included the obituary for Brother Josh. Those were sad yet uncomforted moments.

Not only did Dollee write me, but she enlisted the letter writing of the loving and supportive black women from St. Paul Church who were a part of our chosen family. Sometimes they also sent tokens of their love for me. I knew, without a doubt from their letters, I was loved beyond measure. I remained on their hearts and in their prayers, even when we did not share geography. I learned quickly that relationships amount to more than a common location and bloodline.

19

Skin Folk Ain't Always Kin Folk

Upon arrival at Walker's, I looked for friendships similar to those I left at home. I knew I needed the love and support of others if I wanted to be successful there, so I looked to the skin folk (other black girls) to become my kin folk. And while they often referred to us as "The Family," we were not family. There was no real love amongst us like I experienced at home. While we were of darker hues than the white girls at Walker's, I learned a difficult lesson that "skin folk ain't always kin folk." I also learned that family dynamics determine ways of living together and getting along. Families are what the individuals choose to make them.

Most of the young black children I knew growing up had experiences similar to mine. For instance, most of my friends went to church regularly. Several of my friends also took piano lessons and participated in recitals. And just about everyone had a speech to say on special occasions at her church. We knew because we sometimes practiced them at school. No one's parents were rich, but Nick's grandfather owned a local business in town and his mom had an office job in the federal building downtown, so that made him better off than the rest of us.

At Walker's, with the exception of Paige, a middle-class black girl from Hawaii, we were all in the same proverbial economically disadvantaged boat. Paige was not an ABC student and had a partial scholarship. She had come to Walker's for her senior year of high school. The rest of us were the privileged poor—privileged to be there, yet poor all the same.

No one had any money, not even chump change that we could use as leverage as having more than someone else. We worked the menial jobs in the dining hall or at the school switchboard answering telephone calls for Mrs. Plona, the switchboard operator. What set us apart though were our previous experiences, values we learned at home, and our family background. As it turned out, mine were quite different from those of some of the other black girls. Growing up in St. Paul Church made a bigger impact on my life than I realized. I valued progress and middle-class ideals more than some of the other black girls that I initially encountered.

That was a wake-up call for me in ways I had not imagined. Most of us reside in homes thinking other folk our age live similar lives. That is rarely the case. When you share space living with others who are not your kin folk, you learn a lot about the personal habits of others that you have no right, influence, or power to change. You must learn how to live with those who inhabit the space with you. I had to learn how to live with strangers who resembled me in some ways, but who were not like me in a myriad of other ways. That included practical jokes.

***

Nothing is ever funny if everyone is not having fun. I detest practical jokes. They are not funny, and they are alternate forms of bullying. At least, that's how I felt on two separate occasions when I returned to our room from study hall.

All first-year students attended study hall four nights during the week to make sure that we were on track and to get help if we needed it. Junior and senior girls were paid to proctor the two-hour study hall and to offer assistance when needed. One night, when I returned from study hall, only one of my roommates was in the room. Mary had gone out that evening. I don't know how she did it, but she went on a date on a school night. That was practically unheard of, and it was with an older guy who drove his own car and who was no longer in high school. That was not the astonishing part. What ticked me off was that, when she returned later that night, she walked in wearing my clothes. She had on my brown, low-waist, hip-hugger dress, my black leather coat, and my black leather boots. She had been out getting it on with some guy in my clothes. I was appalled, but she waltzed in with a smirk on her face as if to dare me to say something. I knew I was up against a bully, and I told her, "I don't let other folk wear my clothes."

"I know. You didn't let me. I did it on my own," she retorted.

By then, I was fuming mad. How dare she take my clothes and wear them like they were hers? Anise sat on her bed watching to see what would happen next. I knew that no matter what happened or how wrong Mary was, Anise would side with her. After all, I was the new girl and had not yet earned the right to stand up to them. But I knew I had to say something, even if it caused trouble for me.

"Please don't ever do that again. You can't just take other folk's stuff and use it like you want to. That's wrong," I explained.

Mary simply turned, sucking her teeth. She went into our closet and took off my clothes. We were never cool again, and I knew then that we would never be friends.

One of the situations that happened with the black girls at Walker's was that we all sat together during breakfast and lunch. Dinner was a different matter because we sat at assigned tables for a formal meal with a head of the table and an assigned server. No matter what at lunch and breakfast, it was understood and expected that all the black girls would sit together. After all, we called ourselves "The Family," and families eat together to the exclusion of others. It was a poor attempt at maintaining a sense of unity and camaraderie because while it meant we were together, it also meant there were other girls who we never got to know and develop meaningful relationships as friends. So, as a family, it also meant we were supposed to stick together, participate in the same activities, wear our hair the same way, and look out for each other. That mindset was a form of isolation, control, and manipulation that advantaged some within our group at the expense of others. The incident with my clothes did not seem like the type of thing a family member would do to another member of the same family, but it was a by-product of, and indicative of, the manipulative and intimidating ways of some group memberships.

A second incident happened after study hall. An unsuspecting me went in to use the bathroom one night after I returned to our room. When I sat down, I knew something was wrong. They had greased the toilet seat with Vaseline. I could hear Anise and Mary snicker and then laugh aloud when I jumped up from the toilet. When I turned around and looked at the toilet seat, I saw that they had also covered the toilet bowl with plastic wrap so that whatever my body deposited into the toilet bowl would be caught in the plastic wrap. Fortunately, for me, there was nothing in the plastic wrap. That night as I was taking a bath, Mary decided that, since I took a bath daily (unlike her), maybe I wasn't getting clean enough. She came in and sprinkled Comet bathtub cleanser all over me. I thought, how cruel and thoughtless. I wondered why anyone would be so mean and cruel to me. I had not done anything to anyone to deserve that treatment. I knew she was getting back at me for standing up to her.

As a teen in a new place, I knew I was out numbered and being mistreated. I did not have a friend I could call and tell what happened, and I certainly could not call home. It was taboo for a black girl to tell a white girl that the other black girls had mistreated her, and I certainly could not tell the house parents. What would they do? Move me to another room? That would not have worked. And although I felt betrayed by black folk who were supposed to help me become acclimated to my new environment, I felt as if I had nowhere to turn. I was on my own far away from people who I knew loved me.

That night, I cried quietly in my pillow for what seemed like hours. I let the tears roll silently down my face and gather at my chin. I wept silently underneath my covers. I knew they had gotten the best of me, but I refused to let them see or hear me cry. No way, no how. As I silently sobbed, I felt a glob of phlegm swell in my throat. Although I wanted to go spit it out, I would not dare let them see me crying, so I swallowed it in disgust but with some of my pride left intact. That night, I soaked my pillow with tears.

It was a painful time I will always remember. I understand how taunted and bullied young people feel when their peers, who are supposed to be their friends, mistreat them. Humans are wired to desire a sense of belonging wherever they are. That was all I wanted at Walker's with my roommates. It was my first experience in learning that everyone who looks like me and who is my age is not for me.

I experienced loneliness for the first time. At home, I always had Buster to call on as a friend, and he was not nearby. At other times, I knew that I could talk to Jimmie or Dollee. Long distance calls were costly, and since I didn't have any money, I couldn't call friends back home. I felt disconnected because I was. I shared space with two other black high school girls from economically disadvantaged backgrounds, but I felt isolated and alone. These skin folks certainly were not my kin folk, and I yearned even more for a connection and a confidante. Connecticut had proven to be cold in more than one way.

That night, I silently wept for me and my situation and for the powerlessness that I felt over my own possessions and space. I wept the kind of tears that give you a headache because you've cried so long. I wondered again if I had done the right thing by coming to Walker's. I was isolated geographically, socially, and now, emotionally. When my brain and body could no longer withstand the weight of the painful and tearful emotion, I succumbed to sleep. My roommates never knew nor cared about the pain they caused me, and I didn't speak of that night to anyone for months.

I wonder how I survived and how I made up my mind to stay at Walker's. I know I was not the only one who experienced bullying or taunting there. That is the nature of human beings, especially immature teens whose brains have not yet fully developed. There was something within me that I could not explain that made me want to stay. It wasn't that I needed to prove anything to anyone else, but I had to prove to myself I could handle whatever came my way. And I did.

20

Double Consciousness

Her uniform pristinely white, and her white oxford shoes polished and buffed, Dollee strode to the bus stop to begin her trek to work each weekday as a domestic. City buses picked up other black women dressed similarly whose dreams were buried six feet under in some nice white woman's stock pot, laundry basket, or kitchen sink. They worked for families who only used their last names on payday when writing them a check. Last names of domestics were never spoken. By not speaking their last names, employers held captive any notion of dignity and self-worth for these poor and black women in the work environment. To address them as Miss or Mrs. would have given the black women value, dignity, and worth and acknowledged a level of humanity comparable to theirs. Those families were unwilling to embrace those ideals.

Sunday mornings at St. Paul Church, however, was a time and place where all the black men and women were addressed as mister or missus. Unlike the work week when they were called by their first names by white adults and their children, these folks garnered the respect that was due them on Sunday mornings. The black church was the one place where black adults were respected and addressed as people worthy of dignity and grace. Miss Doris Pendleton (Dollee) served as superintendent of the youth Sunday school. Dollee's true talent exhibited leadership abilities at church. As superintendent, Dollee served on committees that administered Christian education activities and programs. She helped develop the church calendar, planned and prepared meals for the missionary society, and with her lifelong friend, Mrs. B.B. McGhee, they organized the morning worship with scriptures and hymns printed on legal size worship sheets. Words to those hymns and scriptures carried me through my years at Walker's.

One of the perks of attending a school like Walker's in the 1970's was housekeeping services. Each day, nice white women domestics came to our rooms and made our beds, vacuumed or mopped the floors, emptied our trash, changed our towels, and cleaned our bathrooms – toilets, tubs, and all. When nametags were sewn into our clothes, they washed our clothes, too, and returned them to our rooms in neat little bundles. Up until that time, Dollee and other black women in Pine Bluff were the only domestics I knew.

Many of the white girls at Walker's came from families that hired poor and black women as domestics to clean up after them, cook, care for their children, and do their laundry. I was not accustomed to that type of service, so I found it difficult to surrender all of those tasks to Walker's domestics. Jimmie and Dollee taught me how to take care of my physical needs and how to clean and cook. While at Walker's, I surmised that the school provided the domestic services because they wanted us to focus on our studies and not have to worry about cleaning and doing our laundry, but that was not the case. The services were provided so the privileged girls could maintain the lifestyles to which they had become accustomed. *They needed* housekeeping services.

I noticed that the white girls always took the liberty of calling the domestics, dining hall workers, riding directors, and grounds keepers by their first names. Never mister or missus so-and-so. In fact, these workers didn't even have last names printed in the yearbooks. It was as if they had so little human value that they were not worthy of a last name. Calling an adult by her or his first name was just not proper form for me coming from a black community in the South. That's what white people in the South did to belittle black people and keep them in their places. I couldn't do it. I just couldn't call adults by their first names, no matter what role they served. Jimmie and Dollee taught us to be respectful of all people, especially those society would call "the least of these."

At home we learned how to treat other people, no matter who they were, and if we were not old enough to have given a person their name, we had to address them as mister, miss, or missus. I knew the little children of the family for which Dollee worked called her by her first name, and I knew in my spirit as a child, something was wrong with that. No child is supposed to call an adult by her first name without her expressed permission, so I couldn't call the workers at Walker's by their first names. And since no one ever spoke their last names, I usually greeted them without calling their names at all. Ever polite, I treated them with dignity and respect, the same way I wanted Dollee and Jimmie to be treated. I didn't have the heart to do otherwise. I carried with me that double consciousness at Walker's. I was among the privileged, but I never forgot from whence I had come. I knew the plight of other women and girls who looked like me and who hailed from families like mine, and I understood that they, too, deserved better opportunities and more respect.

Dollee spent nearly all of her working years as a domestic. When I left for Walker's, she was with the third and final nice white family. Although she prepared meals, cleaned, did their laundry, and kept their children, they never paid her what she was worth. Not one time did she complain because she said she agreed to do the job for what they paid her. This family loved her and wanted the best for her, but their love did not resemble the love that Jimmie and Dollee showed me.

Like many domestics of her time, Dollee's work ethic was subversive. She performed every task with a spirit of excellence – she never took shortcuts, she worked hard, and she loyally served the families for whom she worked. Although she served in a domestic position, she, too, was aware of the double consciousness of being black in America.

21

The Jams

Kenneth Gamble and Leon Huff were music geniuses and producers of some of the hottest songs of the 1970's. They produced music for some of the top singers of that era, and many of the songs went to the top of record charts. Music coming from Gamble and Huff under the Philadelphia Records label became known familiarly as The Sound of Philadelphia (TSOP). Recording artists under this label included Harold Melvin and the Blue Notes featuring Teddy Pendergrass, Billy Paul, The Spinners, The O'Jays, and the in-house group MFSB (Mother, Father, Sister, Brother). The music was unique and carried with it soulful rhythms and tunes that moved my soul, stirred my body, and roused my feet. I had to dance when I heard it wherever I was. Everyone tapped, bumped, or hustled to their music with hilarity. We boot scooted to TSOP. The music became so popular that a dance show adopted TSOP as its theme music.

Soul Train came on a Hartford/Springfield television station every Saturday afternoon. TSOP played as the show opened, and the black girls at Walker's gathered in the Beaverbrook living room in front of the school community's shared television set to watch it. If another girl was watching television, we convinced her that Soul Train would be a much more entertaining show. Reluctantly, the girl would agree to surrender her rights to television viewing. Inevitably, the other girl would leave the living room before the end of the show. I'm sure girls left because of a lack of interest in the show, but most left because we were so loud with our comments and animated in our practice dance moves.

There was a reason for our intense interest in watching Soul Train. We wanted to see and learn the latest dances. Dancers performed new routines on the show, especially during the Soul Train line. We watched to see what Daveeta Jo was wearing and which dance moves she showcased. Soul Train gave us ideas for what to wear to dances with the boys and the dances we performed.

Walker's staff knew that to be healthy we needed to have healthy interactions with teenage boys, so they planned dances with boys' schools. The black student groups at various schools also sponsored dances and invited black students from other prep schools. We came from schools all over New England and upstate New York, and we wanted to impress one another. Most of the black and brown students were also ABC students. A few came from middle class families who paid either all or a portion of their prep school expenses, but most of us were privileged poor.

In preparation for each dance, there was serious wardrobe planning and dance practice. We made haltered tops from long scarves and swatches of fabric. Taking our tips from Soul Train, we planned the dances to be performed and how we would get partygoers into a Soul

Train line. Initially, it took me longer to learn some of the line and group dances. Learning the Westminster Bop took an entire Sunday afternoon. The Texas Hop took another one, but I got it. I practiced the dances in privacy in our bathroom, hoping to master the steps instead of stepping on my own feet. We practiced those dances with each other until everyone knew what to do and how to do it. We ran circles around our dance partners and everyone, even the guys, got a kick out of watching us.

The most important aspect of attending the dances was what we wore. Our ensembles consisted of a haltered top, hot pants, baggy pants, stylish knee boots, a blazer, and a referee's whistle to make party noises. We would leave Walker's looking presentable with the hot pants underneath the baggy pants and the blazer covering the haltered top. On top of all of this clothing was a heavy coat for the New England cold weather.

A houseparent from Walker's drove us to and from the dances in a school van. One night, Mrs. West, the associate dean of students, was our driver. Previously, married couples, who were Walker's staff and who lived on campus, had taken turns driving us. Before we left the school, Mrs. West asked to see what we were wearing. Proudly, we opened our jackets revealing our haltered tops. With her expression, we thought she would pass out right then and there. She immediately demanded that we change into something more presentable. We resisted, and one of the senior girls stated the case for our attire. She concluded with the suggestion that we get the opinion of one of the male house parents who was also the Dean of Students.

Mr. Pallio and his wife were house parents at Beaverbrook. They had a four-year-old daughter named

Kim, whom they adored, and so did the entire Walker's community. We strutted into his office that evening.

"Their clothes are inappropriate, and they need to go change," Mrs. West announced. "I have tried to get them to put on something different, but they refused. I don't want to take them to the dance dressed like this."

We stood there with our hands on our hips in front of Mr. Pallio with our blazers drawn back so that he could see our outfits. A little smile crept out of the corner of his mouth, and he looked down at the papers on his desk.

Some of us were endowed from the Father with shapely full figures. I was not one of them. Soaking wet, I weighed about eighty-five pounds, and there was no endowment for me. Nothing. In junior high school, I was called stick woman because I did not have hips, a hefty rear-end, or voluptuous breasts (AA cup if you please). Mr. Pallio's eyes went to the shapelier bodies.

He cleared his throat to swallow the grin that wanted so badly to cover his face. His eyes met ours.

"We think these outfits are just fine," explained Mary. "After all, we have on blazers to cover us."

"But are you going to keep on the blazers?" Mrs. West inquired.

"Yes!" we all chimed in truthfully. While we knew we would keep on the blazers, they should have been asking us about keeping on our baggy pants.

What neither of them knew was that underneath the baggy pants were hot pants. While we entered a dance fully clad in baggy pants and blazers, midway through the dance, we retreated to a ladies' room and took off the baggy pants, exposing the hot pants and knee boots. Then, we returned to the dance floor. From then on, we had the full attention of all the males in the room, and we danced the night away until our driver appeared at the door. Then, we put on our baggy pants before we left the dance.

Occasionally, we played tricks on our drivers. When the driver arrived and located one of us, she would tell us it was time to leave and ask one of us to find the other girls. We were never ready to go, so whoever got the message first, let the other girls know, and we danced away from the door so no one could find us. Undoubtedly, it was another thirty minutes or so before the driver found another one of us. This activity went on for about an hour until we could no longer play that game.

Mr. Pallio looked down at his desk, then at Mrs. West, and finally at us. I am sure he had to weigh his decision against the fact that she was his colleague, and any decision that he made could cost him. He looked at us again swallowing that smile and thinking about the best solution. Then he said, "Their outfits are fine. Let them go."

We let out a group roar so loud, girls who were watching television in the living room came out to see what was happening. Mrs. West's face turned light pink, then beet red, and lastly, purple. She was one hot, nice, white woman whose decision had been vetoed by her boss in favor of a group of black girls right in front of them. Once the color left her face, and she returned to her normal complexion, she huffed and walked toward the door. That night, we snickered all the way to the dance. Mrs. West did not say a word.

A few years later, Mr. Pallio was accused of sexual misconduct with a Walker's student.

22

The Invitation

Auna was a friendly white girl who took to me on our first meeting. Although she was a ninth grade student, she was in my French II class. Sometimes we chatted after class. Our conversations were friendly talks about Walker's. I thought she wanted to talk to me because I was so reluctant to speak up in class. Unlike my translation French class at Southeast, Walker's class was immersion, and the expectation was for us to read French literature and think and discuss it completely in French. We read *The Little Prince, Around the World in 80 Days, The Plague*, and a collection of fairytales in French. I knew the Cinderella story, but it was then that I learned that Cinderella or *Cendrillon* means one who tends the cinders of a fire.

I thought I was fairly good in French, but Mme. Moss proved me wrong. I never knew what to say because I had only done basic French verb conjugations at Southeast. So I was quiet in class. At Southeast, we never had authentic conversations in French. The rapid-fire way in which Mme.

Moss spoke was so foreign to me, I could not wrap my brain around it. It was like she was speaking in an unknown tongue without the benefit of having an interpreter. And by the time I figured out what she said, she had gone on to another thought or phrase that was equally foreign and difficult to translate. Instead of thinking in French, I was steadily trying to translate French into English, then back into French so I could make an utterance. That took too much time and did not work. In French class, I was even slower of speech. In any case, Auna befriended me and comforted me after class. She made positive comments about the class and encouraged me.

Auna's parents were middle class, but they did not seem to be as wealthy as some of the girls' families who had the brand names to go with their wealth. There were some family names that indicated the family business or the father's position; whether a senator, ambassador, or businessman with a type of product or company that bore the family name, we knew who was really rich. I'm not sure Auna's family had that kind of money, but they were rich in other ways.

Once or twice, Auna sat with me at lunch at the table with "The Family." Because she seemed friendly and demure, no one bothered her about sitting with us. The invitation came after lunch one day.

"Hey, Veda, would you like to go home with me for a weekend?" she inquired.

I smiled my friendliest smile, thinking this girl who did not look like me wanted to spend time with me outside of Walker's. "Well, I have to get permission from my mother, but yes, I think I would."

I never thought about the potential fallout from this simple decision.

Walker's policy was that girls had to secure written permission to leave the campus when unaccompanied by school staff. That meant I had to get Jimmie's signature on a form indicating that it was okay for me to go home with Auna. It meant mailing the form home, having Jimmie complete it and mail it back to me before I could leave campus. I was willing to go through all of that for a weekend visit with Auna and her family. I wanted another opportunity to feel as if I belonged and was accepted for who I was.

Her invitation excited me. Someone was including me and not asking for anything in return. She wasn't asking me to take an unspoken yet expected oath of loyalty to be with her, to sit with her, or to take part in other activities with her. It was an innocent gesture, and it certainly pleased me.

Auna's family was rich in kindness and generosity. They knew that true kindness knows no shame. There were several children in the family, some biological and some were adopted. Their adopted children included a little black girl. She was a lot younger than Auna, and her family adored her. Auna wanted me to meet her little sister.

I always believe in the innocence of every act, and I choose to believe that folks are just being kind to me with no strings attached. I trust first, and if someone shows me otherwise, it's at that point that I put up a guard. With Auna, I saw no need to put up a defense. She was kind to me, and I had no reason to mistrust her or to question her invitation. I sent the form home to get Jimmie's permission to spend the weekend with Auna's family.

The signed minty green form arrived in the mail about a week later, and I turned it in to Mrs. West who kept up with our whereabouts on weekends. Everything was set, and my excitement began to build as my eyes bounced, and

I clapped my hands. I had no idea what to expect at someone's house, but I was eager to go. In my excitement, I hadn't remembered to ask about the family pets. I knew I was going somewhere to see another place and meet new and different people. I think in my heart of hearts, I was looking to yet someone else to help me become more acclimated to Walker's. Perhaps a friendship with Auna would help me adjust better. After all, I wasn't so sure that all would ever be well with my skin folk.

A final notion I neglected to consider was the reaction of the other black girls to my invitation. Never in my wildest dreams did I think it would matter to any of them. I had not thought about any ulterior motive Auna may have had in extending the invitation, nor had I considered what it might say about my accepting her invitation. I thought it was a kind gesture, which deserved a kind response. My innocence was obvious, and I believed her invitation was both kind and sincere.

"Auna invited me to go home with her for the weekend," I shared with Jackie, "and I think I'm going. My mother returned the letter giving me permission to go. I am excited."

What followed rocked my world, and I had to take a step back.

"So, is that why you wear your hair like that?" she inquired.

"What do you mean?" I asked.

"Straight! Is that why you wear your hair like that? You want to be white?" She pushed and walked away.

Her words stung me like the yellow jackets did one time too many as a child. They cut me to my soul. Her comment stunned me. Never had I considered a response like that. Yes, my hair was straight, but that still didn't mean anything about my blackness or my character. I didn't understand why anyone would say something so hurtful. I was simply wearing my hair the way I wore it at home. No one I knew wore an afro. Everyone wore straight hair in Pine Bluff. I was hurt, but I had to straighten my face and go to lunch.

As I sat at lunch that day, a lot ran through my mind. On one hand, I just wanted to belong…somewhere…. anywhere. I wanted to feel accepted and able to fit in, and I wanted to make new friends. Auna seemed like the perfect candidate for a new friend, yet she was white. That really didn't matter to me, but I guess it was an obvious line that black girls didn't cross at Walker's. My stomach turned during lunch, and I didn't talk much. I ate quietly wondering what I would do. On the other hand, if I went home with Auna, I would probably be ostracized by the black girls. If I didn't go, Auna would be disappointed, and I would have to explain to Jimmie why I didn't go. It was a difficult situation for me, but I had to make a big girl decision whether I wanted to or not.

I let my thoughts simmer in my head a few nights. I knew that I needed the right words, but no words seemed appropriate or honest.

"Veda, are you going?" Auna inquired a few days later. "My parents were happy to hear that you want to come. They need to know how to prepare for the weekend."

I hesitated. Her parents? Why were they happy? What were they thinking would happen? If I tell her no, then her parents will also be disappointed. My heart became heavy. I wanted to go, but what would happen to me once I returned? I thought about this all night long for several nights. Even in my prayer time, I asked God about what was right for me to do. No answer. No warm and fuzzy feeling that would indicate which was the right choice. Nothing. I awoke that morning still uncertain, confused, and wondering what to do.

"I can't go," I blurted out. "I just can't go." There was no easy way for me to turn down the invitation. I wasn't trying to be rude, but in my teenage understanding, I knew I just had to say something, even if it was the wrong thing.

"Why? What happened? I thought you had permission and everything was okay."

"I just can't go," was all I could muster. I turned and hurriedly walked away. Auna hung her head with a puzzled look on her face. Her eyes filled with water at the emotional surprise of my response, and I could no longer look her in her eyes. She couldn't understand why I had changed my mind so suddenly. None of it made any sense to her.

It didn't make sense to me either. My response was painful for me, too. My heart longed for the courage I needed to give her a different answer, but I could not summon any courage in that moment. I had never rejected an invitation. I was torn. Had I done the right thing? What had I done to a potential friend? What sacrifice had I made to be with folk who I wasn't sure really cared about what happened to me? Should I go and apologize? And if I apologize, what good would that do? What would I say? What words would I use and why?

I felt horrible and ashamed, because I had been unkind. I didn't know how to do the right thing. I hurt someone who was just trying to be nice to me when I wasn't sure that the black girls would be nice. After all, three of the six black girls had already shown me how they felt about me. They had been unkind. Was I setting myself up for more pain and humiliation from them? I chose conformity over my true feelings.

Turning down Auna's invitation made French class a little awkward. It took a few weeks before Auna and I could look each other in the eye again. I hurt her by my rejection, and I was hurt because I caused her pain. She and I were both losers, and the winner was Jackie who really didn't give a care about either of us. Her comment was part of controlling the members of the group. Unfortunately for me, it worked that time.

By Christmas vacation of that year, the relaxer had worn off and new hair growth coiled from my scalp. Managing my hair became more challenging with each shampooing. Occasionally, I wore cornrows Kelly, another southern black student, braided for me. When I didn't have braids, I sported a curly afro which I styled while my hair was wet with pink spongy foam hair rollers. Once I got home for the vacation, my hair stylist, who had given me the relaxer months before, cut and shaped my hair into an afro. I had done it.

***

I learned later that Jackie and most of the other black girls at Walker's had never been invited to go home with any of the white girls. In its own way, the absence of such an invitation demonstrated another form of rejection and of not being included or fully accepted as a Walker's girl. We were outsiders. As a result, most of us never formed lasting relationships with the white girls. All of us lost in not getting to know each other.

23

Nullas Horas Nisi Aureas (No Hours Unless Golden)

I magine living in a place and space that is completely foreign to you. Imagine a place where the values in the community are similar to yours but still different. That is what I experienced when I entered Walker's, a place with values that would help further develop my character.

As a child, one of Jimmie's cardinal rules was "Do not lie to me. If you lie, you will steal." Dishonesty was despised at all costs in our home, and if we were caught in a lie, we had hell to pay. Lying and stealing were right up there with cheating. She told us about folks who had cheated on papers and tests and the consequences they suffered as a result of their dishonesty. She said, "Cheating is stealing." I learned about cheating in seventh grade when I let someone copy my homework. I was just as guilty of cheating because I gave that person something that she had not honestly earned. That incident put the fear of God in me, and I vowed to not ever cheat again.

Nullas Horas Nisi Aureas (no hours unless golden) was explained to us in the first school assembly. Walker's had an honor code by which we were to live. Ethel Walker first established the honor code in founding the school in 1911. Cheating of any kind was not allowed, and if a girl was caught cheating on anything, she was immediately expelled and sent home for good. Each girl was expected to complete her own work. If a girl was caught cheating, the assumption was that there was a character flaw in that area, and she had probably cheated in previous work and gotten grades she had not earned.

Samantha Owens was a year younger than me in school, but like some of the other girls, she took courses above her grade level. For instance, World History was a course for sophomores, but first year students like Samantha took it. One day after completing her world history quiz, Samantha decided to read aloud the answers to the quiz while the teacher was out of the room. We were to uphold the honor code in the absence of teachers and school staff. Once Samantha began to read the answers aloud, everyone in the class became obligated to report her honor code violation. Another girl reported it to the teacher, and by the time the rest of the school found out she had cheated, Samantha was already at home. Her expulsion, quick and immediate, let the rest of us know the gravity of her infraction in our school community and that they would not tolerate this kind of behavior. When it came to dishonesty, Walker's was a place of zero tolerance. The school's swift and immediate action left an indelible impression on the rest of us and warned us of our fate should we attempt a similar reckless action.

Cheating never crossed my mind. First, I believed I had earned a spot at the school, and cheating was not necessary for me to remain there. I believed enough in my own work ethic and capabilities to be successful at Walker's. Most importantly, though, was the fear of God Jimmie had instilled in me before I left home. Lying, stealing, and cheating were unacceptable character traits, and I could not bring shame to my family based on those. All my time at Walker's had to be golden according to Jimmie Pendleton's strict honor code. This was one place where there was true intersectionality between the life I lived in Pine Bluff and the one I was now living at Walker's.

***

Each girl had a different purpose for being at Walker's. We had different conceptions of who we were as teen girls and what we were capable of becoming. I thought each of us earned her place at Walker's in the same way. I didn't know there were different processes for admission depending on other factors such as family income, legacy, and social status. In my naiveté, I believed each girl went through the same academically rigorous process I endured prior to admission to the school. And although I went through that process to prove my mettle, it was often assumed that each white girl had earned her place to be there. My admission to Walker's was clearly through the front door, but there were other doors through which admission was gained for some of the white girls. There was no one who could buy my way into Walker's. I had to earn the place I got on my own.

The fact that there were multiple ways of gaining admission to Walker's challenges the notion of *golden hours*.

24

Teacher Expectations of Student Achievement

hen I was a student in Pine Bluff, my teachers held high expectations for me. Even with the recent integration of public schools, my teachers grew to expect work of high quality from me that resulted in top grades, and I demonstrated my ability to meet whatever academic challenges presented to me. I was able to keep up with the best of the students and shine. I thought the teachers at Walker's would automatically think of me as a capable student with brilliance to share in their classrooms. Because the school had given me a scholarship to attend, I thought they expected me to be awesome. Wouldn't they want me to be exceptional and demonstrate academic prowess?

Brilliance and greatness were not what Walker's teachers had in mind when they saw me. Not all the teachers were convinced that I had truly earned a position at the school regardless of my talent exhibited through my grades, teacher recommendations, and test scores. I was simply another poor little black girl they were attempting to "save" from my economically deprived background so that I could be prepped for a world dominated by white decision makers. After all, coming from my background, how could I possibly compete with the more affluent white girls who had every advantage over me? I believe that, in some of their minds, they thought they were doing me a favor by allowing me to be a part of the Walker's community. It was a time and a learning environment in which we were expected to learn from them, but not for them to learn anything from us.

Mr. Provost was the exception. I quickly forgave him for the behavior of his dog, Sebastian, who barked at me every chance he got. In the classroom, Mr. Provost was a caring teacher who took delight in teaching biology. His detailed lessons showed his passion for science, and he always prepared engaging hands-on activities for the lab experience. In his class, I learned about genetics, Punnett squares, inherited traits, and DNA. Those lessons left me wondering about my own DNA since I knew very little about my father's side. It also made me wonder about what, if anything, was unknown or unspoken in my family's DNA and medical history.

It was in the lab on blood types that I became even more curious. As a child, I was always afraid of the prick of a needle, so that day, I had to summon all the courage I could muster to prick my own finger. The pain was less than I had anticipated, and Mr. Provost smiled his toothy smile at me. My blood seeped slowly into the little tube, and Mr. Provost tested it for my blood type. He looked up at me from his microscope and said, "I've been teaching for many years, and you are only the second student I've ever had to have this blood type. Yours is AB-."

"So, what does that mean?" I asked.

"It means you have the rarest blood type."

"Is that good?"

"It's not necessarily good or bad. It does mean you probably got one gene for the A-type from one parent and the gene for the B-type from the other parent."

"Well, I know my mother has B blood type. She also has sickle cell trait. What exactly does that mean?"

"First of all, let me tell you that with AB- blood, you are what's called the "universal recipient." That means you can receive blood transfusions from people who have A, B, O, or AB blood type. Your Rh factor is negative instead of positive."

"What does that mean?"

"That means the Rh or Rhesus factor is not on your blood cells. Rh is a protein on the surface of blood cells of people with positive blood types. You don't have that protein," he said.

"Can that be changed?"

"No, it can't. It's a part of your make up from before you were born. And while you can receive all those different blood types, the blood must not be positive. You need Rh-negative blood. So, young lady, you're pretty rare," he explained.

What I hadn't noticed was that everyone in the class had paused from their own blood typing to listen to our conversation. I was a rarity in this class in more ways than one. I was something special, different from the rest of my classmates. I was the only black student in my class, and here I was with the rarest blood type.

"And, oh, the sickle cell thing with your mom, do you know what that is and where it comes from?" he asked.

"No, I don't. Will it kill her?"

"No. If she only has the trait, it probably won't kill her. It's the people who actually have the disease—sickle cell anemia—who sometimes die from it. Let me explain. Red blood cells are supposed to be round. Sickled blood cells are shaped like a sickle, a tool used to chop tall grass. When the blood cell is shaped like a sickle, not enough oxygen gets to the blood, and sometimes those sickled cells rupture or burst and block the flow of oxygen. That's what makes people with the disease sick. So, the trait alone is not deadly. And sickle cell disease is usually found in people of African descent."

"Okay. Do I have anything to worry about?

"Well, it depends. On the rare blood type, I think you're okay. Just make sure that if you're ever given blood, it's Rh-negative. With the sickle cell trait, you might want to get checked yourself, and make sure the guy you marry doesn't have sickle cell disease or the trait. That could be tough on any children you have."

That day, I learned a lot about myself as a human being and the warm blood flowing through my veins. It was also a day that my teacher learned more about me, and my classmates learned they had a rarity in their midst. It was a lifelong learning experience which helped me be an informed advocate for my own health and wellbeing. Mr. Provost gave me a valuable gift.

Mr. Provost also gave me the gift of high expectations. Throughout the school year, he repeatedly showed me that he believed in me and my abilities. He saw my potential and encouraged me on every hand in every assignment. I'm grateful for the interest he showed in me. He never knew that his support carried me through that year as I made emotional and social adjustments to my new school. He expected me to achieve at high levels, and I lived up to his expectations. That made all the difference in what I learned from him and was able to achieve. It was an emotional turning point for me.

Mr. Provost set the standard for my future expectations of biology teachers. No one I know has had a biology experience like the one I had at Walker's. No one has ever mentioned having a biology lab experience like mine, nor a teacher as devoted to his students' learning science as Mr. Provost.

25

Math Wiz Not

She rode her fold-up bike down the hill to Beaverbrook. Her tight dark brown curls fanned in the breeze. All the girls said she reminded them of the wicked witch in *The Wizard of Oz*. Growing up, I had not been a fan of the witch scenes in that movie and left the room when that part appeared. I was afraid of witches. It's funny how white girl humor is so vastly different from black girl humor. Wicked witch is not the moniker I would have ascribed to her; I would have chosen a noun that rhymed with witch.

Her wardrobe consisted of below-the-knee pencil skirts in solids and plaids, button-up white or pastel blouses and dark-colored flats. Sometimes she wore an elbow length shrug, cardigan, or blazer as a cover up. She wore cat-eye glasses. I often wondered how she rode a bicycle in a skirt, but she managed to do it with grace.

Ms. Tregillus was my geometry teacher. Coming from Southeast, I thought I was good in geometry. Mr. Smith made it seem easy because of the care he took in teaching and explaining geometric concepts to us. That was not the case with Ms. Tregillus. In her class, I got my first dose of low teacher expectations, and therefore, low performance on my part. I gave her exactly what she expected from me.

Geometry became my worst class in high school. It seemed I could never understand geometry in terms of the theorems and postulates I was supposed to learn and use. None of it made sense to me, and it would be years before I understood how all of that was supposed to work to solve geometry problems. It didn't help that my teacher, after the first test, assumed I should not be in her class or at the school. I was constantly humiliated and made to feel as if I were incapable of learning geometry. Unfortunately for me, it was a year-long course, and I had to see Ms. Tregillus at least twice each week. Although I hated the class and the experience, I went to class religiously hoping to glean something from her hurried notes on the chalkboard. She talked faster than she wrote, and because she was ambidextrous, when she reached her limit writing with her right hand on the board, she would pick up her left-to-right progression of notes and continue writing with her left hand. I always left class more confused than when I entered. Was she teaching? Perhaps she was, but not all students were learning, because I was not. I didn't know what I was supposed to learn about angles from theorems, proofs, and postulates.

The teacher-made tests continually stumped me, and I always felt as if I did not have a chance at being successful in her class. She expected the worst from me, and that's what she got, my worst. Until her class, I had never made any grade lower than a B-, and that B- was in seventh grade mathematics when I was learning ratios. That year, with Ms. Tregillus, my math grade tanked in her class, and it never improved. I lived down to my teacher's expectations. And although my mother was not happy, she did not contend with me about my grades at Walker's the way she did while I was in public schools. I ended the school year thinking I was incapable of understanding geometry and doubting my ability to do well in mathematics.

***

I have often wondered what would have happened if my teacher had taken the time to differentiate her instruction just a tad so that I could have learned more. I had access and opportunity, but my teacher didn't know how to reach me where I was, and then teach me in a way that would get me where I needed to be in order to fully participate in discussions and experience success in her classroom. I have also wondered what could have happened had I felt comfortable enough to seek her help or that of my peers. I had never needed academic support to lift my grades out of that depth of mire, so even asking for math help was foreign to me. Those who could have possibly offered help were too busy with their own affairs to tend to me and mine.

Ever since, geometry has posed a challenge for me. It's amazing what one perceived failure can do to the mind and one's actions.

26

Meal Prep

Many schools are filled with policies, practices, and traditions that are supposed to protect us, to nurture us, to grow us, connect us, and build precious memories. Walker's was no different. There were plenty of activities tied either to a policy, practice, or tradition. One such practice was milk lunch. On weekday mid-mornings between classes, a snack of various types of milk, crackers, and cookies was prepared for us. We gathered in the common area outside the smoking room in front of the bookstore to refresh ourselves. Because I have never been a person who eats breakfast on a regular basis, a mid-morning snack was just what I needed to get me through my day. I got my sugar fix, eating Oreo cookies and drinking milk. I sampled some of the other cookies, especially the oatmeal cookies and graham crackers.

Another tradition probably linked to policy was dinner meals. All girls were expected at a sit-down dinner in the dining hall each weekday night. Each table had eight to ten places, and every table had a "head of table" and at least one server. Each girl was assigned to a table, but not an assigned seat. Upon arrival at our table, we had to stand behind our chairs until the head of table said it was okay to be seated after the prayer. The head was a member of the school faculty or staff, or a senior who held a leadership role. The rest of us could be assigned to serve. These assignments were posted weekly outside the dining hall doors. Everyone had her preferences for table mates, but at dinner, that did not matter. We were expected to exhibit our best table manners and engage in polite table talk about school, politics, or our social lives. Sometimes we talked about sports, especially if a school team was having a good season.

Once seated at the table, the server immediately got up and went to the kitchen to fetch the food. Alice, who managed the dining hall, met each of us with a smile and a dish containing the night's entrée. Once the entrée was on the table, we returned to the kitchen to get the side dishes, which usually consisted of a carbohydrate and a green vegetable. The head of table then served the entrée as we passed plates around the table. If we ran out of food, the server took the serving dish back to the kitchen for more. The servers also brought dessert to the table.

I realized that my home life prepared me for these meals. While we didn't have a lot of fancy foods, we ate together as a family and discussed the day's news and events. That's also where we talked about school and learning. I dined with adults at home and learned about table manners and appropriate table talk. Some topics were taboo.

It was during those meals at Walker's, however, that I first tasted yellow wax beans, mashed acorn squash that resembled sweet potatoes, and peppermint and coffee ice cream. Only one of those, the coffee ice cream, became one of my favorite desserts.

We were expected to remain at the table until the meal ended. If anyone needed to leave before the meal was officially over, she had to get special permission from the head of table to be excused. When I first heard of needing to get permission to leave the table, I thought about the dinner scenes on *Leave It to Beaver*. Dinner was one of many traditions at Walker's, which I enjoyed, even when I was the server.

***

"What did they get this time?" Walker's girls often raided the school's kitchen. They stole food after the dining hall closed. I heard about the raids, but never took part in any of them. I was curious about what they stole, but usually by the time I heard there had been a raid, the perpetrators had disappeared and so had the food. None of the black girls ever participated in the kitchen raids out of fear of retribution or even dismissal. We knew there was little room for us to make an error. I am certain the kitchen staff noticed the food was missing, however no one was brought up on charges of breaking the school's honor code for raiding the kitchen. Perhaps it was considered a white-collar crime, an innocent prank, and was an exception to the school's honor code. It was vandalism and theft.

27

Cicerone

I never thought of myself as an introvert as a child. I was always talkative. I talked about everything to anyone who would listen. A neighbor had labeled me as "that talking black gal." I was more comfortable in my skin than most of my peers, more confident in my abilities, and I didn't mind telling others about it. By all accounts, I described myself as gregarious and excited about life and learning. Much of that changed in my Walker's world.

My presence at Walker's began to challenge everything I knew to be true about myself. Our first few days of school rendered me reticent in my classes. Uncertain of my responses or of appropriate content, I shied away from raising my hand in class and made attempts not to be called on by teachers. And while I completed my homework assignments at Walker's, I was never quite sure of the quality of my work. That was not a consideration in Pine Bluff.

Socially, I became more withdrawn. While I continued to sit with the black girls at meals, I knew in my heart they would never be lifelong friends, only acquaintances at best. I knew I was wired differently for a host of reasons, but I felt unable to fully become who I was because I chose their companionship, however insincere, over my true self. I knew that I was a kinder, gentler person who wanted to grow and learn more about other people and about the world. As I grew less and less into who I really was, I became more introverted. I searched inwardly for some other self who would embody the traits that would be comfortable with these girls, but that self never surfaced.

Although I was still searching for myself and for my place at Walker's, I decided to become a cicerone. A cicerone is a tour guide who shows prospective students around the campus and explains as much about Walker's school life as one can in a short visit. Cicerones work with the admissions office and conduct campus tours when they fit into their schedules. Sometimes student visits include more than simply day tours, and girls stay on campus overnight.

After spring break my first year, I returned to Walker's and learned that a prospective student would be coming for an initial visit. Liz Henry asked me if I would be interested in hosting her for a couple of days. She would stay in our room, go to classes, and share meals with us. I agreed to host her.

My guest arrived in a taxi the same way I did, all by herself. Hailing from the South Bronx, she arrived for a Walker's tour. Like many other ABC students, her academic prowess was recognized, and she was tapped to participate in the ABC program and possibly attend Walker's. For her time on the campus, I was her cicerone.

Nyoka Delphina Browno strutted into the Beaverbrook lobby full of confidence. Weighing in at seventy pounds and five feet tall, she walked with extreme confidence. I, on the other hand, did not walk that way, and my lack of confidence at Walker's was beginning to show in my rounded shoulders. At least, I thought it was showing.

"Hi, Nyoka, I'm Veda. I am your cicerone for your visit," I greeted her.

"How are you? And what's a cicerone?"

"It's just a fancy name for a tour guide."

"Oh, so how long have you been here?"

"This is my first year."

"Well, how do you like it so far?" she asked.

"It's okay," I lied. In a sense, it wasn't a lie. There had been some good moments, but I was still struggling. Struggling with homesickness. Struggling with my new environment. Struggling with geometry. Struggling with my roommates. Struggling with a lack of genuine friends.

"Just okay? This is a pretty fancy school for it to be just okay," she responded.

"I know. We'll talk about it later. Let's get some lunch."

I didn't know who I was trying to convince about my life at Walker's, me or Nyoka. In any case, she noticed my ambivalence in ways that the other girls had not. It was as if she had a sixth sense and saw the real me. The hurting and longing me. The me who had become unsure of who she was and who had turned inward for self-preservation and protection. The me who liked connecting and getting to know others. The progressive thinking me. It was as if in a few moments she had seen it all, and I knew it.

I introduced Nyoka to the other black girls at lunch. They greeted her cheerfully. She was a hit with them from the start. My roommates doted on her and were friendly. I watched them wondering what the difference was.

I took Nyoka to my classes. That afternoon we went to tennis. I had begun playing tennis in the fall. The tennis coach was nice to the black girls. She was young and had signed on to be an advisor for most of us, including me. It would be my senior year before I would break rank and choose someone else as my advisor.

I was slowly learning how to play tennis, and it was becoming a joy to hit the balls. Our coach made a big deal out of my left-handed shots and my ability to hit backhand shots. Like me, Nyoka had never played tennis. In the South Bronx, she played handball. I had never heard of handball, but she assured me that the volleys in handball were comparable to those in tennis.

The girls reserved a seat for Nyoka at dinner that evening. As usual, the white girls were quite gracious and encouraged her to come to Walker's. I smiled sheepishly at their encouragement and wondered what they thought the Walker's experience was like for anyone other than themselves. Did they have any idea what it was like to be a black girl at Walker's? Did they know how it felt to be the only person of her race in classes all day long? Did they notice the stares that I got from each of them, their collective eyes glaring at me when questions about black people were hurled in my direction? Surely, they didn't, simply because they didn't have to be pensive about their existence in the world. They could just be who they were as white girls growing up with privilege in this country. That was not the case for me, and no matter how I dressed in their uniforms or prepped for the world beyond Walker's, I would still remain a black girl in America fighting for a seat at the table of justice and equity. I knew that, and they did too.

W. E. B. DuBois wrote about the double consciousness of black people who live in America. Unlike white people in America, blacks can never afford to *just be* and relax in our skin. We have an increased awareness of our citizenship that whites rarely, if ever, have to think about or consider.

We are black, and we are American. Most whites simply think of themselves as American. Being black in America always has a *double entendre* because of the stigmas, stereotypes, and biases often associated with our presence here. Although blacks are stereotyped in various ways, too many times we prove that the opposite is true.

My experiences at Walker's continued in that same vein.

After dinner that night, I had an opportunity to share with Nyoka my real feelings about attending Walker's. I shared with her some of the stories about what had happened up to that point with me.

"So, Veda, where are you from?"

"Pine Bluff, Arkansas."

"Where's that?"

"It's next to Oklahoma, but under Missouri, near Mississippi."

"Well, I'm not good with geography. So that didn't tell me much."

"Okay." I shrugged thinking about all my geography lessons at home and at school.

"And why do they call it Arkansas and it's spelled like Kansas? Shouldn't it at least be Ar-kan-sass or Ar-Kansas? I'm going to call it Arkansass."

We both fell out laughing.

"Well, I guess it could be, but I think it's an Indian name and pronunciation. At least, that's what I remember from eighth grade Arkansas history."

"So, when I asked you about your time at Walker's earlier today, I felt like there was something else that you wanted to tell me."

I knew it. I knew she had picked up on my true feelings and was now asking me to explain them to her. I decided to follow my heart and let it all out.

"Well, since you asked, it's been tough. Anise and Mary are buddies, and they hang together all of the time. It's been hard living with them. They've pulled all kinds of practical jokes on me, and I hate jokes and pranks."

"Oh, no! For real? What did you do? Who did you tell?"

"I didn't do anything, and I didn't tell anyone. Who would I tell?"

"I guess you're right about that. What are you going to do? Are you coming back next year? Let me know before I decide to come here."

"I don't know. If I come back, it will be hard. If I don't come back, then they will win."

"Hmmmm?"

"The hardest part is that I don't have any friends here. Jackie is my "old girl," and even she hasn't always been kind. I guess it's hard to make friends at Walker's. What do you think I should do?"

"Well, if you come back, I will come to Walker's, and with both of us here, I will be your friend."

That night she slept on the floor beside my bed. I offered to exchange places with her since she was my guest, but she declined.

Nyoka meant every word of her statement. Before she left for home the next day, she gave me her Bronx address. I enjoyed writing letters, but I wasn't sure about her interest. We agreed to write to each other over the summer. She was going to the Williams ABC Program in June, and we agreed to write more after that event. She was true to her word, and so was I.

28

Summer Breeze

The summer between my sophomore and junior years was uneventful. There was no welcoming home from friends or family. There was no summer job waiting for me. In fact, after applying for several jobs, I gave up. Every employer wanted to know what Ethel Walker was. When I told them it was a prep school, they simply shrugged and filed my application away somewhere. They had no reference for what a prep school was, and certainly had no plans to hire a young black girl who did not attend a local high school.

No one ever asked about my learning experiences or social life. No one asked about the teachers and how they treated me at Walker's. Most of the black males wanted to know what it was like to go to school with all girls, especially mostly white girls.

"Ain't some of them 'funny?'" One asked.

"Funny" in those days was a term used, especially in our community, as a polite term to refer to gays and lesbians. So, in asking the question that way, this young man had not intended to offend anyone. He, like a lot of other people, imagined what a single-gender school might be like, and he was being as polite as he knew how to be.

"It's not like that," I assured him.

"Well, why would all girls want to go to school together without boys?"

"Why not? There's an all-boys school across town. We get to see them on weekends and at parties. School is just a lot easier with all girls. And we are just friends," I continued to explain.

"I don't know about that." He shrugged and walked away to play basketball with Buster and some other boys.

That summer, I attended a few dances at St. Peter's Catholic Church, the black church in Pine Bluff located on the east side of town. They held Friday night dances for black teens in the community. Buster and I went to the dances together. Going with him and not a friend of my own was one of the first signs of my oncoming estrangement from my previous friends.

Going to Walker's had begun to cost me some valuable friendships. Perhaps it was just me, and these changes were a part of growing up. I'm sure others also changed friendships over the high school years, but my relationships with my friends seemed to have been a casualty of leaving Pine Bluff. Fortunately, at the dances, I danced my way to a good time.

When the music started, I took to the floor and began doing one of the dances we practiced at Walker's after watching Soul Train. Producers did not broadcast the show on Arkansas television networks, so every dance I did was fresh and new to my audience. Sometimes, I danced alone for an entire song. At other times, a brave guy joined me on the floor. When that happened, I danced circles around him to showcase my skill. The other folks who knew me stood back and watched, some shaking their heads, while others gawked. I sported a large afro, and my tops were usually one of the haltered or midriff tops I made and wore to the dances on weekends at Walker's. I didn't dare wear hot pants to St. Peter's, but wore baggy pants and platform sandals.

Lorie was the only friend who would come by the house to talk to me. Although she was in Buster's grade, we spent hours in our driveway talking about everything. She was an "A" student, but she said she was never leaving home to go to school, and she kept her word on that. Like the boys, Lorie had lots of questions about prep school, or college as she called it, but she always had encouraging words for me. She alone got to hear some of the struggles I had at Walker's and how tough some of the classes were. She heard about boyfriends and other friends. Eventually, we grew as friends, and every time I came home, she dropped by our house for a casual conversation.

I was an anomaly in my own hometown, and I was beginning to feel it more and more. It was as if I no longer fit at home or at Walker's. I was a poor, southern, black girl who was having the educational experiences of a rich white girl. It was as if I had no solid friendships in either place. And I was expected to play two roles, depending on where I was. Each role had to be played appropriately in each environment. I had to code switch not only my language and habits, but my entire being as well. I had to culture switch. At home, I had to be "Veda from Pine Bluff, Jimmie's daughter," and at Walker's, I had to be a Walker's girl who happened to be from the South. Talk about bewildering. I felt like I didn't fit in at either place. I knew up front that there would be changes, but losing my former friends was not one that I had anticipated. Marion had remained friends with his Southeast classmates after going away to prep school and then to Princeton, and they always hung out together when he was home for breaks. What happened to me and my friends?

And although I was at home in Jimmie's house, as the summer wore on, I yearned to return to Walker's to a place that had become familiar to me. For nine months, I lived and breathed that environment, and I longed to get back to that space. It wasn't that I was eager to undergo the same experiences from the previous school year, but my longing was filled with hope and the expectation that the environment would change so I could begin to grow into my own person with the love and support of a new friend. I was prayerful and hopeful, and the universe did not disappoint.

29

The Return of the Not-so Native

A 1970's black male trio called Black Ivory sang a song called "Don't Turn Around" about not ever turning around and continuing to look forward, and although the song was about a love relationship, it seemed appropriate as a theme song for me and my return to Walker's for my junior year. I could not turn around and retreat from the opportunity. The name Black Ivory is an oxymoron, and my attendance at Walker's seemed like that, too.

Nyoka, Kim, Karen, and Lynn. And just like that the black student enrollment at Walker's bounced back. Four black seniors graduated in May 1973, and four new black students arrived on campus. Nyoka, Karen, and Lynn were from New York, and Kim was from Washington, D.C. They were all big city girls. Nyoka was a junior like me; Lynn was the lonely only black sophomore; and Karen and Kim were the ninth-grade black students (Karen wouldn't make it past the first trimester.) Lynn and Nyoka were the two ABC students, and Kim and Karen were on partial scholarships.

Lynn arrived just like I did with bags in tow all alone. Her mother thought she could make the trip by herself, so she let her ride the bus from the City into Hartford. Nyoka's mother and friend, Mr. Lincoln, drove her, and Kim's mother and her friend, Mr. Lacy, drove her up to Simsbury from D.C. Kim was an only child whose father had died in a work-related accident. We stared at her room when we saw all the creature comforts she had brought with her. Most of us had clothes, toiletries, and a clock radio, but she had a stereo with records, both forty-fives and long play vinyl and separate speakers. We were curious about her possessions.

Karen came with her entire Barbadian family, including her brother, Ronnie, who attended a nearby boys' school. Karen was the youngest in her family, and we soon found out that she liked to be petted and to have her way. I knew that wouldn't last long at Walker's, but she had to find that out on her own. Although we collectively continued to call ourselves "The Family," we were anything but that. No one was going to care for or tend to Karen like her family did. We were teenage girls without fully developed brains, and we had not yet developed the compassion needed to care properly for one of our own. We were too busy caring for ourselves and starring in our own lives to do that.

Nyoka and I were roommates and were assigned a suite in Cluett Hall. There were two bedrooms with a sliding wooden door in between. That gave us an opportunity to talk to each other or to close the door for privacy. Our door remained open, and later we made one room a study room and put both beds in the other room.

Walker's traditions were strong. Upon arrival, each girl was assigned to a side/group of the school. You were either a Sun or a Dial, as in sundial, the school's symbol. I was a Dial. There never seemed to be any rhyme or reason as to why someone was dubbed either a Sun or a Dial. School colors went matched the groups. Suns wore yellow and Dials wore purple.

Another Walker's tradition was the Old Girl-New Girl Show. The school encouraged all girls to participate, but I never did. I didn't feel as if my piano skills were good enough to display; I couldn't sing; and dancing was not something I wanted to showcase in front of teachers and peers. I never considered reciting a poem. Performing in front of folks I really didn't know was not appealing to me, but I was pleased when others performed, especially the funny skits that poked fun at the adults.

Nyoka, Kim, Karen, and Lynn performed a dance routine to "It's a Thin Line Between Love and Hate" by The Persuaders. I had heard the song, but I didn't know all the words, and I certainly didn't know the meaning of the lyrics. They dressed in black slacks, dress shirts, neckties, and blazers to resemble The Persuaders. Their performance was cute, but Nyoka had to explain to me later that the man was singing about how his wife treated him after he spent the night out with another woman. I later wondered why four black females would want to perform such a song.

Two white girls streaked during one of the acts. Masked with pantyhose, they dashed in the nude across the stage. We cheered!

I pondered my "why" for returning to Walker's. I had to return. Staying in Pine Bluff and going to school there was no longer an option for me. It would have been nice to remain at home and be with my family after a tough first year, but more and more, I was beginning to feel as if I didn't fit in my community. I knew that, because of my learning experiences, even though they were challenging, I was no longer fit to consider attending Pine Bluff schools. Returning home would also have meant I had failed, and that was not a choice for me. I had to try Walker's again, so I returned for another year.

30

Me and the Boys

Aaron Franklin Thomas attended Deerfield Academy. We met at a Deerfield dance during my first trimester at Walker's. He was a tall, lanky, ebony brother from New York City and knew ABC students from the City. We danced together all night on that first meeting, wrote each other letters several times, and talked about meeting up at other dances. He even called me a few times. Then, suddenly, there was nothing. No communications whatsoever. I wrote letters and called the pay telephone in his dorm. Nothing. I tried everything I could to contact him, but there was no response. My heart hurt because I thought I had found someone who liked me. I was wrong. His lack of a response weighed heavily on me and became a distraction from my schoolwork. I didn't know what to do or to think. He ghosted me. Months later, at another dance, I saw some of the Deerfield guys. I cornered a guy named Blaine and asked about Aaron.

"So, where's Aaron?"

"Well, nobody told you?"

"Told me what? What happened to him?"

"He's okay. He's just back in New York."

"Why is he there?" I wanted to know.

"Well, it's a long story." He signed.

"I've got time. Our van leaves later."

"Well, some of the guys had been taking things that did not belong to them," Blaine began.

"You mean stealing?"

"Yep! Stealing."

"So, what did he steal?"

"Well, another student reported that his expensive watch was stolen. Then, the student who had lost the watch saw his watch on the sink in the locker room. Someone had taken it off and left it there while taking a shower. The guy decided to wait and see who came back for the watch. It was Aaron. He couldn't deny stealing it because he knew his family couldn't afford that watch. After they caught him, they kicked him out of Deerfield."

"Oh, my goodness. When did all this happen?"

"It was during basketball training season. The coach was really interested in him playing. He has a nasty hook shot like Lou Alcindor. He would have made a great player, but he's back at his old school in New York."

"I guess I was spared a thief."

"Yeah, you were."

Our first dance of junior year was in October. Young men from different schools attended the dance. As usual, black students scouted out other black students. We needed to connect with folks who looked like us, who may have had hair like us, and who had similar struggles and goals as ours. We looked for familiarity in each other, and we wanted to see black and brown males who might be interested in us. That night breathed new life into my time at Walker's.

Hotchkiss School in Lakeville, Connecticut, was an all-boys school close to the New York state line. A few of Walker's students were familiar with the school because they lived in Sharon, Connecticut, close to Lakeville. Hotchkiss boys filled the gym at the dance. Once we scouted the black guys, we left the dance and took them to Cluett's living room. Anise and Mary set up their stereo, speakers, and records. We had no idea who these guys were, but we thought we'd get to know them away from the crowded gym and away from the eyes of onlookers.

We performed our Soul Train dances, both line dances and dances with partners. After we danced until we perspired, someone played a slow jam, a tune by the Temprees, "This Is Dedicated to the One I Love." Everybody's movements slowed. All the girls partnered with someone but me. Neither had Kabrian Browne. He came over and sheepishly asked me to dance. I smiled and agreed to dance with him. The closer we got to each other, the more our perspirations mingled. He wore a black leather jacket and black platform shoes, a 1970's unisex phenomenon. The platforms helped Kabrian. He was five-foot-six with a big afro, a huge smile, and wire-rimmed glasses. He had muscles, lots of them.

"So, where are you from?" he asked.

"You promise you won't laugh if I tell you?"

"I promise."

"I'm from Pine Bluff, Arkansas. It's the second largest city in Arkansas."

"Oh, okay. How big is that?

"About 50,000 people. Where are you from?"

"I'm from L.A."

"You mean, as in Los Angeles, California?"

"Yes, that's right."

"How did you get all the way out here?"

"I wanted to go to a school where I could play ice hockey, and Hotchkiss was it. Plus, they gave me a scholarship to play ice hockey."

"You play ice hockey? Isn't it hot in California?"

"Yep!"

"So, how do you play *ice* hockey there? And who ever heard of a black guy playing ice hockey? I thought only white boys played ice hockey."

"I do, and I like it. And I am the only brother on our team."

"Don't you get cold on the ice?"

"At first, but once you start skating, you warm up quickly."

"How did you get started playing ice hockey?"

"They have teams in L.A. for little kids, and I started when I was nine."

"Oh, okay."

"Enough about ice hockey. Let's listen to the music."

As we listened to the Temprees confess their desires for love, I felt Kabrian snuggle a little closer to me. The music carried us to another place, and our thighs began to touch as we moved slowly to the music. The better the music got, the closer we moved together. And then in a surprising move, he did it. He sneaked a kiss. And as we continued dancing, we kissed each other. It was on then! I never thought I would fall so quickly for anyone, and because of his actions in the days and weeks that followed, I knew he felt the same.

For the rest of that night, we danced only with each other. Eventually, we stopped dancing and sat on the sofa and talked. We discussed school and what it was like at prep school. He said there were ten black males at Hotchkiss, but not all of them attended our dance. They had a black male advisor. I lamented that there were no black adults at Walker's and that we had to look to white staff for guidance. We decided to exchange mailing addresses and telephone numbers. No one had a telephone in her room. We took turns using the pay phone at the end of the hall. Thankfully, the phone was housed in a booth-like room that allowed for privacy.

The night ended with what would be the third of many demonstrations of affection. We were smitten with each other and would be for some time. I had entered my first real teenage relationship, and it felt so, so good.

31

Prepped for What? – Part II

Rita K. Shea was an historian extraordinaire. A graduate of Radcliffe College, she held high expectations for herself and for her students. She was a nice white lady who was unafraid to speak her mind and kept up with local, state, regional and national politics. At Walker's she taught American History, and many of the girls yearned to learn from her. So, it was a shock to me when I appeared in her class early on the first day of class in my junior year only to find that I was the only student in her class. There was a scheduling glitch because of my piano lessons, and Mrs. West enrolled me as the only student in that section of her class.

Mrs. Shea was aware of the situation, but I wasn't. It became really clear to me that, since I was the only student in the class, I would be expected to answer all of the questions. I would always have to be fully engaged in a discussion with the teacher. Up until that point at Walker's, I had been the reticent student, answering only when called upon. Being the sole student in the class would not work for me. She and I discussed her expectations for the class and how we thought things might go with just one student. We agreed that I would probably learn more if more students were in the class. We also agreed that I would stay in the class and give it a try. As soon as the class ended, I went promptly to Mrs. West and got my schedule changed, dropping the class with a plan to take it during my senior year. I was not about to put myself through that.

During my junior and senior years, I took piano and flute lessons. My piano lessons were with Rosi Grunschlag. She and her sister Toni were Austrian pianists who lived and worked at Walker's. Rosi was the more serious of the two sisters while Toni was the jovial one. My lessons were therapeutic and refreshing because we played classical duets, and sometimes spent the entire class period sight-reading pieces. We enjoyed those lessons. She was pleasantly surprised at my skill level, and so was I. She was able to bring out of me what Mr. Moore prepared me to do.

My flute lessons were a different story. Walker's paid for my lessons, but I traveled by bicycle on a three-mile trek to the teacher's home, a nice white lady in the community. I borrowed another girl's bicycle. Although I enjoyed bike riding, it was quite a chore traversing the curvy hills of Simsbury on the edge of the narrow road with a flute in the basket. At points along the way, I dismounted and pushed the bike up the hills and around the curves. I never considered my personal safety traveling alone to a flute lesson or wondered what might happen to me out there by myself. I took it in stride as another lesson in developing greater independence and self-reliance. It was reminiscent of my traveling alone to piano lessons in Pine Bluff.

College planning conversations began early at Walker's and we prepared for college entrance examinations. We took the SAT and the Achievement Tests in English and mathematics. The first administration of those tests took place at the school in the same room as study hall. The fall of my junior year, we took the PSAT. High scores on that test meant attracting the attention of colleges and universities. We were also encouraged to sit for multiple test administrations to boost our scores. Everyone at Walker's knew that multiple attempts produced higher scores simply because of the practice and preparation involved and increased familiarity with the content of the tests. The school prepped us for the final test administration, which would be during the fall semester of our senior year. They knew the proper preparation had to be done over time with coaching and practice for us to perform at high levels. That made a lot of sense, especially since that is how anything that is done well happens. It takes continued practice and intentional preparation over time.

I sat for multiple administrations of all the tests. I wanted to do well. I knew and understood the impact of those test scores on college admission decisions, and I wanted to ensure that I had the best opportunities available to me when I applied to college. Sometimes I took the tests at Little Rock Central High School during breaks and vacations. Little did I know at the time the potential impact of the testing site on test performance. The result was that with practice, my scores improved.

As a result, I became a viable candidate for selective colleges, but not Ivy League. Attending an Ivy League college was not on my radar; I just wanted to go to a good college. I was prepping myself for opportunities to attend a reputable college preferably on the east coast. I had no idea which college that would be, but I was confident that I would go to a respectable college. Walker's staff wanted to see each girl go to college, and some members of the faculty were willing to counsel and to direct us.

Formal talks about college with Walker's girls and Mrs. West began early because Walker's wanted us to begin thinking about what we'd like to become and then choose a college that offered a program that would prepare us to achieve that goal. Each girl chose an advisor to help in this process. The black girls as a collective group had chosen the same person to be their advisor. Miss Sue was from a small white town in the northeast. Her background in dealing with black girls was limited, and like many of the other white faculty and staff, she held low expectations for us. She had good intentions, but that was not enough. It was what I now know and recognize as implicit biases that have the potential to hinder the progress and achievement of economically disadvantaged students and students of color. It's the little thoughts and ideas about diverse people groups that others often carry, and many are unaware that they even harbor those biases. It's the notions that have developed over time about various people groups that haunt our ideas about them and impact our decisions about how we interact with them. Those biases impact their daily interactions and conversations about diverse groups. Biases---we all have them, but we don't all have the power to act on them.

"So, Veda, what do you want to become when you grow up?" Miss Sue asked me.

"I really like working with children. I have taught Sunday school and babysat."

"But what do you want to do with that interest?"

"I think I would like to become a child psychologist. That way, I could really help children."

"Oh, my! What a lofty goal! I think you should be more realistic in choosing your goals." With that comment, she walked away.

I dropped my gaze, and my countenance changed. Something inside me was attacked by someone who was supposed to encourage and support me. It was one question and one answer that she decided was the wrong answer. She offered no advising type discussion of what it might take for me to pursue such a career or the steps I might take to achieve that goal. The most heart-wrenching part was that she never saw anything wrong with what she said to me. For her, openly dissuading a black girl from having lofty goals and verbalizing low expectations was acceptable teacher talk. We never had another discussion about my college or career plans.

From that point on, my spirit for even thinking about becoming a child psychologist was crushed. Her words were painful and let me know what she really thought about me, and probably about the other black girls she advised. She really did not think I could earn an advanced degree that would qualify me to help children and families. It was disappointing, but it became a sobering moment for me as I began to think more clearly about my possibilities for college and for selecting a college major. I listened to other voices on the faculty, who had a different perception of who I was and of what I could become. It was as if Miss Sue had her fingers in the eyes of the black girls who thought of her as their trusted friend only to find out otherwise later in the game. Maybe, just maybe, Miss Sue wasn't for us after all. Perhaps her job in advising us was to maintain the *status quo*, whatever that meant, at Walker's in the 1970's.

That was her last advising session with me. The next day, I broke rank from the other black girls and chose my chemistry teacher as my advisor. Although I did not have the language at the time to express my hurt and dissatisfaction with Miss Sue, I knew in my heart and in my spirit that her response to me was not what I needed in order to grow and to become all that I was meant to become. I saw it as a put-down from someone who never got to know me as a human being. She had only had me in tennis, and nothing more. She had never seen my writing. Perhaps, it was the geometry grade that gave her pause or that shaped her perception of my capabilities. Perhaps her comments were indicative of the times in which we lived. Although black girls attended Walker's, I am not sure that any of the adults knew what to do with or for us.

***

Like newly integrated schools all over the country in the 1970's, black and white teachers and students were put together without any consideration of how to work together or how to understand each other across racial, socio-economic, and cultural differences. We just had to figure it out the best that we could even if it meant someone would be placed at a disadvantage. I was that someone that day.

I re-grouped emotionally to move forward. In my heart, I wondered what this experience was prepping me to do. I knew that if I ever had an opportunity to help or to give advice to someone, I would do my best to see as many possibilities for her as I could even if she did not yet see them in herself.

Miriam Huntington was a fine academic advisor and a nice white lady. A mature teacher and advisor, she held real conversations with me about my future and about my desires as a young woman. Mrs. Huntington also talked to me about being more deliberate about looking out for myself and being more selfish when making decisions. She supported and encouraged my interests to the best of her abilities, making attempts to understand me and my background. She believed in me, and for that, I am eternally grateful. Mrs. Huntington said she would help me in any way she could, and she did.

32

Exposure

My first Broadway play was *Hamlet*. I read and studied at least one Shakespearean play each year I was at Walker's, but it was getting to see *Hamlet* on Broadway that left a lasting impression on me. A black man played Horatio, and he was a gorgeous specimen in purple tights which matched his purple and green tunic. Oh, how I swooned over that vision of beauty on the stage. And how excited I was to be in a theater on Broadway. I talked about that man's physique for weeks.

Walker's prepped us for the world by exposing us to cultural events. Taking a busload of young women to New York City to see a Broadway play was just one example of the school's tireless effort either to show us the world or to bring the world to us. Invited speakers came to campus and artists performed in the arts center. Even Livingston Taylor, brother of James Taylor, performed on campus. One year, a child psychologist delivered a lecture at Beaverbrook. He talked about Freud and the *id*, the *ego* and the *superego*. He told us that four-year-olds are egocentric and only think about themselves. He went on to say that children do not have a memory before they are four. To prove his point, he asked Mr. Pallio's four-year-old daughter, Kim, to participate in a conversation with him. She proved his point about egocentrism when he asked her to make a choice between something that would directly benefit her in the moment or choose something that might not benefit her immediately. Her choice followed his theory, and we were amazed by his insight.

There were concerts on campus performed by music faculty as well as guest performers. On one such occasion, a conductor performed with his orchestra. One of the pieces that they played that evening, "Cielito Lindo," a popular Mexican tune, contained the melody to what we knew as the "Frito Bandito" song. Every time the orchestra came to the chorus of the piece, Walker's girls loudly sang the lyrics to the Frito Bandito commercial song. We amused ourselves, but irritated the conductor, and his ire with us shone all over his flushed face. He finally gave up, and when they played that part of the piece for the last time, he turned to the audience and conducted our sing-spiration. We got a big kick out of that portion of the concert, but we never realized how racially inappropriate the Frito Bandito song was.

Mrs. Shea kept us abreast of American politics. In assemblies, speakers came and shared their positions on current events. The Vietnam War was the backdrop for much of what was happening, and most of us knew somebody who had either gone to battle or died in the war. And those of us with older male siblings feared that they would be drafted to fight in the war. When the Vietnam War ended, we were summoned to the living room and Mrs. Shea announced that the combat had ended, and

American troops were on their way home. Everyone shouted, hugged, and cried tears of joy.

Mrs. Shea also kept us up to date about the Watergate scandal and its impact on public policy and American government. Fortunately for us, Richard Nixon's impeachment and subsequent resignation came during the summer when we were at home. I watched his resignation and his wave goodbye as he boarded Air Force One on the black and white television set at home.

Walker's exposed us to various forms of athleticism and sports. I learned that wearing a tunic, blouse and bloomers did not prevent us from performing our best in athletic practices and competitions. Except for the girls participating in horseback riding, everyone had to wear the uniform.

Each girl participated in a sport. That was fine for those who were athletically inclined, but for me, it was an adjustment. I began to play tennis my first year. Tennis was offered during the fall and spring trimesters. In winter, I played paddle tennis. The tennis coach encouraged the black girls to play tennis and paddle tennis. I attempted running cross country, but soon quit because of the distance. I was good with short sprints, but I did not have the stamina for long distances.

Jimmie had played basketball in high school, so I decided to play too. In her day, and even in public schools during my time, girls played half-court basketball. Private schools were the exceptions, and we played full-court basketball with a lot of running and perspiration. Sneakers had not yet become a mega-billion-dollar industry. Converse All-Stars (Chuck Taylors) were the rage, and I wore a pair of white high-tops with at least three pairs of socks. For practice, I wore ankle weights so when jumping for the ball without the weights, I would soar, and soar I did!

My only problem with basketball was with my undergarments. After being fitted for a training bra, it would be years before I would have my own bra that was not a hand-me-down. For all of prep school and some of college, I wore the second-hand bras of the white lady for whom my aunt worked. I found it hard to get anything but a training bra to fit properly. Proper fit was not a priority, and I just needed to have my nipples covered. I wore those bras, and without fail during every basketball game, my bra strap would come loose and flap visibly under my arm and out of my shirt. Each time Coach Scarles called a time-out and called me to the bench to fix my bra. At first, it was embarrassing, but after the third or fourth time, I shook it off and saw it as a part of my participation. I don't think anyone owned a sports bra at Walker's. Dance students joked about putting Band-Aids over their nipples to keep from wearing a bra. I laughed with them when I heard their discussion knowing that I could have done the same, and no one would have been any wiser.

As a junior, I earned a spot as a starting forward on our basketball team. Standing at five-foot-six, I worked my tail off in practices, showing an aggressive side in rebounding and defensive plays. Wearing those ankle weights paid off, and I was able to "sky" to fight for rebounds. Coach Scarles decided that it would be a good idea to strengthen our practices by playing some of the male faculty members on campus. We practiced for an hour at 6:30 a.m. several days of the week. Our regular practice time was in the afternoons, and sometimes in the evenings. The men gave us a tough workout, and we had to hustle if we wanted to get in a shot. Luckily, due to our sizes, most of us were faster than they were.

As that season wore on, we became a powerful team, making shots and limiting our opponent's opportunities for rebounds. What happened surprised all of us--especially the team. We were undefeated. Our last game was at home, and as we entered the dining hall that evening, girls serenaded the team with "Hoo-ray, Sun-ray," the school's spirit song. That song is one of strength, unity, support, and encouragement that affirms each girl in her pursuits, be they academic, athletic, artistic or otherwise. A salute to excellence, it is a time-honored tradition that everyone in the Walker's community embraces as an affirmation of its members. As our team entered the dining hall, we beamed with pleasure at our accomplishment. The first undefeated team in the Farmington River Valley in eighty-three years, we were Valley champions.

Whenever I receive mailings from Walker's with the "Hoo-ray, Sun-ray" song and my name inserted, my spirit lifts, and I continue to feel the warmth of Walker's. It is a reminder of a time and place in my life that holds significance and meaning. My time at Walker's was a time of tremendous growth and development, and hearing that song reminds me of all that I learned and earned, about life and myself.

***

It was while at Walker's that I attended my first rhythm and blues concert. Headlined by Stevie Wonder, the opening act was Rufus featuring Chaka Khan at the Hartford Athenaeum. Wearing our jams attire, Nyoka, Kim, Lynn, and I strutted into the venue as if we knew what we were doing. I had no clue what to expect. Darkness and cigarette smoke filled the arena and the music blared. Folks sitting behind us smoked reefer. At one point in the show, they extinguished all the lights and asked the audience to hold up their cigarette lighters. As a non-smoker, I did not own a lighter, so I watched as others held up theirs and waved them. We jammed with Chaka and Stevie like we had never partied before. The concert exceeded our expectations. What a night!

33

"Ever the Best of Friends"

A major reading in eleventh grade English was Charles Dickens' classic novel, *Great Expectations*. No matter whose class you were in, that book was required reading. Robin and Nyoka had their English class together. I was still the lonely only in my English class with a different teacher. The main character in the novel, Pip, whose given name was Philip, was an orphan who lived with his disparaging sister, Mrs. Joe, and her kind husband, Joe. Mrs. Joe was not nice to Pip, but Joe was and thus developed a lasting friendship that helped both manage their lives in a continuously challenging environment. It was a loving and lasting relationship filled with mutual respect, admiration, and kindness. Pip described their relationship as "ever the best of friends."

"Ever the best of friends" is how Nyoka and I grew to describe our friendship. We were polar opposites in so many ways, but that was not a deterrent to our budding friendship. She was from the city, and I was from a small town in the South. She was from a big family with several brothers and sisters, and I only had Buster, LaWanda, and Marion. Her parents had been married to each other, and mine had not. And although she had a strained relationship with her father, at least she had one. She was light-skinned, and I was truly blessed with lots of melanin that gave me a rich dark chocolate hue. She described herself as not having any color. I was tall and lanky, and she was petite. She was a thinker and reminded me that I needed to be one also. I was an optimist and always looked for the best in others while Nyoka had real life experiences and was a realist. She often said that I went through the world wearing rose-colored glasses, and that was true. I always believed in the good in people first or until they showed me otherwise. There were plenty of differences between us, but there was also enough common ground to unite us in a lasting and loving friendship.

I was a Christian, and she was agnostic, but she often asked me about my Bible reading, prayers, chapel attendance, and what I believed. Not one time did she judge me for my beliefs and practices. I was happy to share with her what I knew and believed it was my job to pray for her as my friend.

She declared herself as geographically challenged, but thanks to Mrs. Worley's seventh grade geography class, I was not. I knew where all the states were, had memorized all of the state capitals, and I had even learned about other countries and their capitals. I was naïve about the world, and she was worldly experienced and wise. She had done and seen things that I had never heard of people our age doing. I learned I had lived a sheltered and safe life. Jimmie and Dollee protected me from as much as they could.

Nyoka came from a home of self-advocacy too. She knew how to stand up for herself. So, when the school did not have any uniforms small enough for her, she requested uniforms in her size. Her request went unanswered until she made a phone call home. She let her mother know that the school had not supplied her with uniforms as they promised. Her mother contacted the school's Board of Trustees, and soon after, they ordered the uniforms. After receiving the uniforms, Nyoka decided they were too long, cut them off, and hemmed them at her desired length.

Nyoka came to Walker's self-assured and arrogant, and walked with temerity. I had come to Walker's self-assured, too, but I quickly found myself in a world of self-doubt and confusion, which resulted in introversion and sometimes timidity. I turned inwardly for self-reflection and self-preservation. I was forgetting who I was and whose I was. I was beginning to build a wall of protection that Nyoka showed me I did not need to have with her.

Nyoka and I ended up living as juniors in Cluett, a privilege given to only a few juniors during their first trimester. We lived on the second floor and shared a suite. We were fine during the first month or so before the Connecticut weather turned brutally cold. I had become accustomed to the snow and the cold, but Nyoka was not, even though she was from New York. Our wooden lever windows continuously allowed cold air to enter through the cracks making our rooms more like meat keepers. LaWanda bought me an electric blanket that kept me warm on frigid nights. During the coldest time of the school year, Nyoka and I decided to put our desks in one room and our beds in the other room. That way we could share the use of the blanket. We got the idea from some of the other girls who may have shared bedroom space for other reasons than for warmth. It was clear to all that Nyoka and I were both heterosexual girls who huddled together for warmth only.

As friends, Nyoka and I spent a lot of time together outside of class. We aptly chose nicknames for each other. She called me "Vee," and I called her "Knikii" (pronounced Nicky) or "Knik" (pronounced Nick). Those nicknames stuck. Whenever Knik and I were not in different athletic classes, we were together. She played volleyball, and I played basketball. I attended volleyball practices and learned how to keep score and help with the team. I also went to all the home volleyball games and occasionally some of the away games if there was no conflict with basketball.

Nyoka and I grew to enjoy each other's company as two black girls traversing a white world at a school for rich white girls. We understood that while Walker's was designed and established for girls, we were not the girls that Ethel Walker had in mind when she organized the school. It was *nice* to some that we were there, but we knew that the school was designed for others. We were being tolerated and not fully accepted, and we understood that. While we were welcomed to the school, many of us never had a true sense of belonging. There were never opportunities for learning or events that celebrated us and affirmed us in our blackness. I don't know if the adults at Walker's knew or wanted to learn about our blackness. They showed us that they didn't care by the lack of actions, assignments, and activities that embraced who we were or that reflected who we were becoming.

We had to figure out how to make a Walker's education and experience work for us as young black women. And since we represented all that blacks do and are in America, we had to be extremely careful not to taint the images our classmates held of other black folks in America. This is always a heavy burden for young people to carry, but one we were able to carry with relative ease as we partnered together in friendship.

Nyoka and I talked about everything. I told her about my life in Pine Bluff, about Buster, and about how he beat me up from time to time as a child. I shared with her that I still loved him as my younger brother anyway. She talked a lot about her boyfriend, Lane, in the South Bronx and how they spent time together. She even knew about gang activity in her neighborhood. That was foreign to me. The closest I could come to understanding anything like that was with the youth chapter of the Eastern Stars and Masons in Pine Bluff, where Buster and I were members. We had colors that we wore on Saturdays and for special meetings. We had secret handshakes and signs that only members knew. Our youth organization paled in comparison to the gang activity that she described.

Despite all our differences, we had the common experience of attending Walker's and of wanting to get a fine education that would change our lives for the better. Walker's seemed like a good place for us to get that started.

At night, our conversations focused on the events of the day and on our interactions with white girls and teachers. Robin came by our room frequently and talked for hours. While acknowledging the injustices that we met, we chose not to dwell on them in ways that would negatively impact our own progress in learning and growing. We had to figure out how to rise above the gross inequities we experienced at the hands of Walker's faculty and staff.

Nyoka was experienced with boys, and I was not. In my relationship with Kabrian, she quietly watched from the sidelines. She knew that I had fallen for him and promptly warned him of his doom should he decide to hurt me. I laughed when she told me she had told him this. I asked, "What do you think he will do to me?"

"I don't know, but I don't want you hurt," she said. She was looking out for my well-being and that act alone endeared me to her even more. Here was someone who cared enough about me as my friend to want the best for me and who was willing to take action if necessary, on my behalf. Up until that time, only Jimmie had done that. Before Knik's arrival at Walker's, I had never experienced that type of friendship, and I hoped I would never lose it.

I had found my kinfolk at last.

34

Equity

Rap artist Gil Scott-Heron wrote and rapped about civil rights issues in America and in urban communities. He, along with other artists like Curtis Mayfield, Nikki Giovanni, and Marvin Gaye, set the musical backdrop for addressing the social and civic injustices that blacks faced in America in the early 1970's. They were *thought* lyricists, who dared to dream in living color and to think out loud about our lives in a better light, a light that would allow all of us to shine in our gifts and to show others the way to a more peaceful and just world. We sang their songs and repeated their poetic words in ways that kept us going even in the face of explicit and implicit biases.

I first heard these artists while at Walker's, listening to the records owned by my roommates. I memorized the words to "Nikki Rosa" and "The Great Pax Whitie." Those words spoke to my spirit and reminded me of who I was as a teen black girl, as a black American and most importantly as a human being living in an unjust society with little power to change any of the injustices. As I listened and repeated those words to myself, I prayed I would live to change my life so my future children would face a different world.

Equity was not a part of the Walker's language in teaching and learning. The word was never mentioned as a concern during the 1970's. The term "equity," at that time, was used to talk about equity funds or equity in home ownership, so even the thought of discussing equity as it relates to human beings was foreign, not only to the Walker's community, but to folks everywhere in the USA. I believe the faculty and staff thought we should be grateful to be at the school and that was enough. At no point did anyone ever ask me if I felt as if I were being treated justly, or if my needs were met. I had no real clue as to how to effectively articulate my needs, academic, emotional, or social in a way that would not be perceived as disgruntled or ungrateful. I knew that as a black teenager, there would always be little room for error on my part, so there were some situations that I had to live with and tolerate because of the times. That was an era when folk thought, felt and believed that you earned what you got by your own hard work. While meritocracy has its merits, it has never been a true reality for people of color and poor people in America. At Walker's, it was an aristocracy cloaked in meritocracy.

We rarely discussed racial relations and civic unrest in classes or in social settings. Even with the backdrop of racial tensions during the 1970's, Walker's faculty and students never engaged in real talk about racial and civil rights concerns. And although the busing problems in neighboring Boston were intense, we never had knowledgeable conversations about them. Perhaps we were all afraid of the feelings and emotions that might emerge if we explored those issues. Maybe we didn't have the appropriate language to properly discuss those matters in meaningful contexts that would help us better understand each other. Our own fears and inadequacies kept us from growing and learning more about life in America for different groups. And there we were, black and white teenage girls together not knowing how to navigate the social and political issues of our time.

Instead of talking about issues related to race, prejudices, and civil rights in America, we went along and pretended as if all was well. There was no awareness of social justice, and even when black girls experienced unfair actions of white girls or teachers, the Walker's faculty and staff were asleep. In their minds and in their worlds, they never had to explore their own biases and feelings about other races. All just went along to get along, and that was not good for the growth and development of anyone, especially the black girls.

Once, while minding my own business in my room at Beaverbrook, two of my white classmates decided to prank me by bringing Sebastian to my room and sticking his head in the door. Everyone knew about my fear of dogs, and yet these girls thought that bringing this dog, who barked at me incessantly and showed aggression toward me regularly, was a fun thing to do. I was both surprised and frightened. I complained to the houseparent, who did nothing. Part of the problem was that the person who heard my complaint owned Sebastian. Since the adult did nothing, I retaliated against those girls. I emptied their trash cans on their beds and told them they had a surprise waiting for them. My actions were then reported to the same houseparent, and I was punished. I was furious, but there was no adult at

Walker's looking out for what was best for me or seeking justice.

I wondered how my punishment could have been the right action to take. Where was the justice? They got this woman who looked like them to affirm them in their devious actions and to condemn me in mine. Had they never pranked me in the first place, I would have had no need for retaliation. What happened was wrong on so many counts.

***

Student leadership was another issue at Walker's. No one ever questioned why student leaders were all white girls. Nominated and elected by the student body, the members of Big Six made up the student governance leadership, but during my time at Walker's, there was only one black member of Big Six. Black girls did not make the cut. After that, and for my remaining time there, no black girl served on Big Six. The Junior Birdman, a school spirit character, was always white, and so was leadership in Grapes, the school's selective choral group. In fact, the only leadership role any of us had was Head of the Athletic Association (AA). No one voted on that position. The position was handed down from black student to black student, because that was the only leadership opportunity we had. It was handed to a rising senior, but the position held no real power or benefits and was like being president of a small school club, whose membership was mostly black.

I was the head of AA my senior year. There were never any clear guidelines for the organization, and I rarely if ever met with the school's athletic director or coaches. We occasionally had club meetings, and the only thing I remember doing was establishing cheerleaders for athletic events. The cheer squad was made up of the black girls and a couple of white girls. We cheered at home games in which we were not participating. Since there was no budget, there were no cheerleading uniforms, no pom-poms, and no organized routines. We just used our voices and cheers that we learned at previous schools.

As a black young girl at a predominantly white all-girls school, I found few if any opportunities for personal affirmation of my value, dignity, and purpose. I felt as if I were tolerated more than accepted. Tolerance means that one simply "puts up" with someone rather than embracing all that the person brings to the environment. I wondered if we were like their pets, seen but not really heard or respected beyond the gleam of the tiled floors of the buildings. We were fed and our physical bodies maintained, but unlike pets, we had human emotions and social needs that often went unmet. We were born to be a bit higher than their pets, but I'm not sure they recognized those needs in us.

They expected us to be different, but those differences were not valued or seen as worthwhile unless someone in class wanted to know how black people did this or that or how black people felt. When those questions arose, they expected black students to speak for the entire black population. They expected us to carry the weight of all blacks and be able to summon an appropriate response that would inform white people without offending them. We were supposed to say what they (white people) wanted and needed to hear. They wanted a version of the truth told in words that would affirm their biases and prejudices and would make them feel good and remain comfortable in who they were. They were white and wanted to always be right even if they had no real knowledge of the topic related to other groups. They wanted to always control the narrative even if it wasn't their story to tell. It was their world that we had chosen to enter, and we had to figure out for ourselves how to maneuver in it. I had not learned polite white speech at home. I had only learned my mother's tongue, and she always said what was on her mind.

I often chose reticence rather than saying something that would make white people feel good about the treatment of black people in this country. And for that, I paid a price.

35

Lacuna

The Lacuna is a time honored Walker's tradition. The term *Lacuna* means a gap or a break in something. At Walker's, the Lacuna is a break in studies. Occurring during the winter months, the Lacuna is a two-week break from regular classes, a time to explore other courses and interests, giving everyone a planned intentional respite from routine school life. I participated in athletic classes like paddle tennis and bowled. I took Afro-American history with Mrs. Shea. "Afro-American" was the appropriate term to use when referring to people of African descent. In that class, we read *Before the Mayflower* by Lerone Bennett, Jr. and explored the lives of black people in North America before the Pilgrims arrived.

I also learned how to play Bridge and found out that it's easier to play than Bid Whist, a game the black girls taught me to play. Bid Whist requires more talent, chance, and thinking than Bridge. I took sewing again (I had taken it one summer in Pine Bluff) and made a black corduroy pantsuit which I modeled for *The Pine Bluff Commercial*. And

I made one last attempt at learning how to knit. My Lacuna English course one year rocked my world.

English teachers offered courses centered around an anchor text or theme. During the Lacuna of my junior year, I became fascinated by a course titled *Coming to Terms with One's Self*. Our anchor text for the class was *I Am A Sensation*. The focus of the class was to explore who we were becoming and who we would like to become as we grew and changed. We were to think about the process in an existential way by giving our lives the 30,000-foot view while living it. The teacher asked us to think about a person whom we admired, research the person's life, and be able to tell the class why we admired that person. We were supposed to get our information from wherever we could, including library books, newspapers, and magazines.

I chose Angela Davis, an intelligent, confident, and fearless, outspoken black woman. Her huge afro let everyone know that she meant business when she spoke, and she represented all that I thought I wanted to be and do. She spoke her piece and wasn't long in doing so. She was unashamed of who she was, and she let everybody know it. I was proud of the woman I saw in Angela Davis. And even though I had read about her *alleged* connection with an attempted prison break in California, I had no idea how close to home her association had been to my teacher's world. I knew Ms. Davis served jail time for her alleged involvement, but after eighteen months in jail, they found no evidence of her involvement and released her. In a sense, she was a *shero* because she beat the charges. That was something few blacks were able to do in the 1970's.

I was thrilled with what I learned about Ms. Davis. I cut out her picture from *Jet Magazine* and posted it on my closet door. I walked into class the day our assignment was due, pleased with myself and knowing that no one else would have chosen the same person. Even though we could choose our classes, I remained the only black girl in that Lacuna class. No one else wanted to read and to work that hard in an English class when there were so many other options that did not require the same level of commitment and effort.

After calling on several of the other girls and listening to their reports, the teacher turned to me.

"Veda, who did you choose to research, and why? Who do you admire?"

"I chose Angela Davis," I announced proudly.

At that moment, I could see the discomfort rising in her throat as the muscles and veins in her neck tensed as she tried to maintain her composure and search for words. She swallowed hard and pursed her lips in ways that people do before they deliver a verbal blow. She could hardly wait to speak. I wonder if she thought about me as a human being as she chose her words. I wonder if she even cared about me as a student or even wanted to know and understand why I made such a choice. Like other girls, I wanted to identify with someone who looked like me, who held similar values and who had taken a stand to make a difference in the world. Angela Davis embodied everything I admired. All I know is that what came out of her mouth that day hurt tremendously.

I went on, "Angela Davis stands up for her people and for what's right for all people, especially for Afro-Americans. She says what she thinks, no matter what. She is not afraid to tell it like it is, and not everybody will do that. I like that about her, and her words are powerful. She is a bold Afro-American woman, who likes herself and all that she represents. I want to be like her."

By this time, Ms. Levy's face had gone through various shades of pink and red and was now *blurple,* and she looked as if she might explode if she didn't get out her thoughts right that minute. Before I could finish my presentation, she had had all she could take of hearing about Miss Angela Davis.

"What do you think you're doing? Don't you know all the harm she has caused? She supplied the guns used at the botched prison break at San Quentin when they were trying to free George Jackson. My friend's father was a guard at that prison, and he died in the gunfire along with four others. So, when you think about someone you admire, be careful who you choose. She's not someone you should admire or want to be like, young lady."

She scolded me and turned to her desk and began nervously shuffling papers. She had shaken herself with her stern attack on me. I believe that in her own heart, she knew she was wrong. Again, she had succeeded in shaming me in front of my peers. A few seconds after her tirade, her painful words reverberated in my ears, and I held back the tears I needed to release so badly.

And with that, my presentation ended. Through cloudy eyes, I looked down at my paper and at the picture of Angela Davis in my notebook. Slowly, I closed my notebook and continued to stare at it. My Lacuna classmates looked at their feet and made no response or noise. It was total silence. No one coughed, sneezed, sighed, or shuffled paper. No one moved as we waited to see what the teacher's next move would be. She did nothing more. She had done enough. The class period ended without further discussion.

The wind left my sail. I thought I was following the assignment guidelines. I did the work and the research and made what I thought was a quality presentation, yet, I managed to offend and upset my teacher. As a student, I had no way of knowing what to think or do. The situation remained on repeat in my head. I questioned myself and my reasons for choosing Angela Davis. The black community revered Ms. Davis for her political stances and outspokenness. She delivered bold and dynamic words that many black people felt and wanted to say. An educated and talented young black woman, Ms. Davis had it *going on* in multiple arenas, and she was a force. Yes, she was radical, but she had reason to be. She stood up to the powers that be and used her voice in speaking out against injustice to make a difference.

I wondered what Mrs. Levy thought of me as a black student in her classroom. Did she see me as *poor little Veda* from Pine Bluff who had so much to learn about white people and what they liked and disliked? Did she see me as someone who had her own dreams and desires, or was I supposed to dream the same dreams as the white middle-class girls? What did she *really* think of me? And no matter what she thought of me, did she care enough to get to know me as a black girl who was growing and learning about herself and about the world and the environment in which she lived and learned? What was her real beef with me anyway? And I wondered, what was this whole situation preparing me to be able to accomplish?

I took my papers back to my dorm room and put them away. No word was ever spoken of this classroom event. Reticence had become my friend and frequent companion, and I turned inwardly for comfort. I had not learned how to pray for myself and for my own healing from hurt. And I certainly had not learned how to forgive others when I was wronged. I only knew how to nurse my pain.

***

I have not held grudges against those who made choices that impacted my life negatively. Instead, I have chosen to walk in forgiveness. I could not afford to let folks get in my head in ways that could potentially lead to my own detriment. I just couldn't, and so I didn't. I understood the era in which we lived and the limitations of human thinking at that time. Our time was on the heels of the Civil Rights Movement, and everyone (Black, white, and other) was left trying to figure out how we should live and behave towards other groups. We needed more time and opportunities to learn about each other, but my teen brain did not have that presence of mind. I still had to know and believe I had done the right thing and had done as the teacher instructed. That understanding alone helped me maintain my sanity and move forward.

The Lacuna ended with a long winter weekend. I spent that weekend with my sister, LaWanda, in New York. I needed a break from all that was Walker's.

36

The Messiah, The Elements and Marvin

My interest in music was piqued long before my arrival at Walker's. Mr. Moore had a lot to do with that as my piano teacher in Pine Bluff. A classical clarinetist himself, he participated in concerts at Arkansas A. M. & N. College. When he thought his students were mature enough to appreciate classical music, he invited us to attend the college's holiday performance of Handel's "Messiah." Mrs. Thomas, my friend Nick's mother, drove the two of us to the campus and dropped us off at the auditorium. The performance was two hours, and she was not interested in spending her Sunday afternoon there. What happened that first "Messiah" afternoon opened my mind and my music interest and took my ideas about classical music to a new level.

That first "Messiah" afternoon, I had the opportunity to see African American musicians display their talents with a spirit of excellence. I saw and heard college students, both male and female dressed in black-tie formal attire sing with clarity, dignity, and professionalism. The choir director,

Shelton McGee, was a member of our church congregation, and he conducted the choir with enthusiasm. It was an impressive event, and I witnessed Mr. Moore perform in first chair.

After that afternoon, I planned to attend the college's performance of "The Messiah" annually. I went to the concert, even if I had to go alone. I enjoyed the music, and I admired the sophistication of the performers, who were my people displaying their talents in ways that demonstrated their giftedness and love for music. I loved hearing "The Hallelujah Chorus." Like King George II, I always rushed to my feet when I heard it.

My fascination with music was further developed by the hymns and other sacred music that I played in Sunday school and church services. I enjoyed learning new tunes, and the better I got at playing them, the better I felt, and the more words I learned as I attempted to sing the lyrics. My interest in music was enhanced by the musician who played the pipe organ at St. Paul Church. Dr. Grace Delois Wiley made the organ sing, and her repertoire was eclectic. While her expertise was sacred music, she played classical music such as "Going Home" by Antonin Dvorak at funerals. It became one of my favorite pieces. I learned that Dvorak valued African American music and enlisted the musicality of Harry Burleigh, a composer and baritone who happened to be African American when he composed "New World Symphony."

Music was a form of release and relaxation for me. When I became irritable and moody due to pre-menstrual syndrome or other frustrations, I played the piano for emotional relief. I gave the piano keys and my fingers a workout. I played all my favorite tunes until I felt relaxed and got myself together. I even played pieces I had not yet mastered to stimulate my brain and to take the focus off of my feelings and emotions. The words to the hymns like "Blessed Assurance" and "What A Friend" kept me focused and comforted me. Playing hymns was limited at Walker's, so I had to find other musical outlets.

Rhythm and blues singers of the 1970's sang about a range of topics. There were plenty of love songs that caught my attention, but the tunes that stood out were by artists like Marvin Gaye, Curtis Mayfield, and Gil Scott-Heron. They sang about the conditions of blacks and poor people in America. Their lyrics caused me to pause and ponder what was really happening to my people post-Civil Rights Movement. Other artists like Stevie Wonder and Earth, Wind and Fire, also known as The Elements, gave words to help us think about what it means to be human in a world that doesn't always recognize and affirm your humanity. Earth Wind and Fire offered solutions to the plight of African Americans during the 1970's. Their songs were about black folks finding ways to love themselves and to love and support other blacks within their own families, homes, and communities. They promoted self-love to impact positive and lasting change.

Songs like "Devotion," "Keep Your Head to the Sky," "That's the Way of the World," and "Open Our Eyes" helped me get through my years at Walker's. Their songs reminded me of the promise that lay within me and that exists in each of us.

Marvin Gaye's *What's Going On?* album challenged listeners to think about what was happening with our children and to ponder the question as to who is really caring for them in songs like "Save The Children," "Mercy, Mercy Me," and the title tune "What's Going On." These songs spoke to the human condition of blacks in both inner cities and rural communities. The writers witnessed the conditions in which we lived and wrote music to address our plight. And although equal rights were secured their words reminded us that, even though we were free, we were still in economic bondage that controlled much of what we did with the rest of our lives. Even with the reality of those social and emotional conditions, their music promoted hope for a better future and life. Their music was not Christian *per se*, but their messages held a spiritual undertone that reminded me of the hymns and spirituals that we sang at church. They used their musical gifts to create messages to uplift a group of people, namely mine.

Artists under the Gamble and Huff label gave us lyrics that articulated civic concerns. Songs such as "Give the People What They Want" and "Love Train" by the O'Jays and "Am I Black Enough for You?" by Billy Paul spoke to concerns in our community. Their songs encouraged black pride and black self-determination in ways that everyone understood and contemplated. The music inspired us, and we needed those words. I especially needed them as I learned more about who I was as a black person, as a female, and as a teen in America. My presence at Walker's afforded me a unique and privileged experience, but even in thinking about what lay before me, I still had to think about my presence there with all of the labels and layers of humanity I carried with me.

These songs aided me in processing my feelings as I grew into the space and place that I occupied at Walker's. The lyrics provided a mental space that gave me the capacity to think more deeply about what was happening to others while I participated in life and learning at prep school. I was angered knowing that what was happening in poor urban and rural communities could be fixed if those making social, political, and economic decisions about the plight of all Americans wanted real change.

Other musicians gave us good, clean love songs about loving another in powerful and meaningful ways. I fell in love with music from the Temprees, a male group from Memphis, TN. I found out that Mr. Moore's brother performed with the group. My favorite song was, "This is Dedicated to the One I Love."

Black Ivory, the Chi-Lites, the Temptations, the Isley Brothers, Harold Melvin and the Blue Notes, the O'Jays, the Spinners and New Birth were popular male groups whose music topped the charts in the 1970's. The men sang love songs mostly in falsetto voices. We swooned over their lyrics. On days when I felt like giving up or going home, songs like "Don't Turn Around" reminded me to continue moving forward.

New Birth and Bobby Womack both sang versions of "Wildflower" that moved me to tears. Their words boasted of a woman who's precious to the crooner and his promises to love and support her in any season. He professes eternal love for his wildflower.

Love ballads like "You Make Me Feel Brand New" by The Delfonics, "I'm Stone in Love with You" by The Stylistics, and "Lovin You" by Minnie Riperton spoke to loving another human being as much as you love yourself. Other tunes by The Fifth Dimension such as "One Less Bell to Answer" and "If You Don't Know Me by Now" by Harold Melvin and the Blue Notes lamented the struggles that lovers face in relationships.

What was so special about these tunes was that listeners could always understand the words-- every word of them. The producers always included the lyrics on a cover sheet within the album packaging for readers like me. The songs ended on notes of hope and redemption. Those words became a part of listeners, and we crooned with the singers whenever we heard those songs. It was those lines that guys repeated in our ears on the dance floor, releasing scents of mints and gum that mingled with the odors of perspiration, cheap cologne, and heavily worn leather.

Then there were the dance and love songs of that era. Stevie Wonder's "Superstition" brought out energetic dance moves in us. I especially enjoyed using whistles in the refrain while dancing. It was the love songs like Stevie Wonder's "*You and I*" that brought me closer to Kabrian, my sweetheart. Rhythm and blues songs of that day spoke of love, an everlasting love with memorable words and tunes that were easily understood. Kabrian and I shared the lyrics from some of those songs in our love letters to each other.

37

Imagining My Heart with You

"**D**id he really hitchhike to Walker's just to see you?" Lynn wanted to know.

"Yes, he said he got a ride with some white man in a truck."

"Wasn't he afraid?"

"That's what I asked, too, but he seemed to be fine with it."

"He must really like you a lot," she continued.

"I guess he does."

It was not unusual for Kabrian to hitchhike a ride to see me at Walker's. In fact, on most of his weekend trips to our campus, that's how he arrived. He got a ride from Lakeville as close as he could get to Simsbury and either hitchhiked again or walked the rest of the way. On my weekend visits to Hotchkiss School, I rode a Greyhound bus to Lakeville, and one of his ice hockey coaches picked me up at the bus station. The coaches loved "Kabe," as they called him, and did whatever it took for him to be happy.

Throughout our junior year, Kabrian and I dated each other exclusively. Our first meeting set off a prep school romance that was intense and full of love and favor. During the week, we wrote love letters to each other telling about our week. Usually, I got two or three letters from him, and he got the same from me. Included in my letters were song lyrics that expressed my affection.

In addition to writing letters, we talked on the telephone a couple of times each week. Each phone call started as paid with enough coins for a three-minute call. Near the end of the three minutes talking time, an operator interrupted and told me how many minutes or seconds remained. Before the end of the call, I asked the operator to make the call a third-party billing. That meant I could talk as long as I liked, and Ma Bell would mail me a bill for the amount of the call. I spent much of my Walker's allowance and work-study money on calls to Kabrian.

Male visitors, brothers of girls and boyfriends, who stayed on Walker's campus spent the night in the basement of Galbraith gymnasium. There were beds and a bathroom with a shower for guests. Girls could not to go to that room, but of course, we broke that rule. Nothing ever happened between us in that space. Someone watched the building on those weekends.

Kabrian and I spent a lot of time exploring some of the 800 acres at Walker's. We didn't cover even half of it, but we did take long walks to talk and to be alone. Because he had a healthy appetite, we always made it back in time for meals. I was in love, so I had no appetite. On one of my visits to his school, I watched as the boys stormed the dining hall in a rush to eat. They acted as if they were famished and hadn't eaten in days as they raced to be the first in line. They ate as if it were their last meal.

At meals and at other times, I swooned over Kabrian's presence, and once he was satisfied, he paid more attention to me. Between and after meals, we often sat in the living room of one of the dorms, sometimes alone and sometimes with other girls. With Kabrian, I felt free to be who I was without putting on airs or trying to be like the other girls. And although I didn't know a thing about dating or being in a serious relationship, I thought I was ready to learn.

Whenever I visited him at Hotchkiss, I stayed with one of his coaches and his family. I slept on lots of sleeper sofas and played with little white kids whom I'd never met. At ice hockey games, I sat with the coach's family. After the first game, it became apparent that I needed to wear warmer clothing and thicker socks. I nearly froze at that first game.

Kabrian was a superb athlete, and repeatedly got hat tricks. I sat and cheered at the games as if I really understood them. I was familiar enough to know when he made a good shot and asked lots of questions. And whenever he got a hat trick, they gave him a gold paper Burger King crown that he passed on to me after the game.

During ice hockey season, if Hotchkiss had a game close by at Avon Old Farms School or another school, someone from Walker's drove me to the game so I could watch him play. The coach always made arrangements for me to get in the games, and I was expected to sit with his family. Kabrian's eyes always found me during the games, and I cheered for him.

I had never been in love, but this felt real. It was genuine. We talked about everything together from school and our dreams to our families, hockey, and tennis. Occasionally, on Soul Train Saturday afternoons, he danced with us. Whenever we walked together, it was a hand holding moment. That was the only public display of affection allowed at both schools, so if we wanted to be more affectionate, we took a walk out of the sight of adults and students.

I was a good Christian girl from the South. Growing up in Pine Bluff, I was sheltered concerning male-female relationships. I learned in seventh grade about human conception. I had only known my mother, so I had no idea how I arrived on the planet. When my affection towards Kabrian increased and his increased for me, naturally I was stumped as to what to do. I knew that I had come to Walker's to get a better chance at life, and I didn't want anything or anyone to stand in the way of that happening.

Over the days, weeks, and months that we dated, we realized that we truly cared for each other and began to use the "L" word when describing our affection for each other. We wrote and said "I love you" in person and on the telephone. The more we talked and saw each other, the more we wanted to be together. And as we worked to get together, the adults in our lives observed our behaviors and continued to support our efforts. For the first time in my life, I began to imagine giving my heart to him, and I did. I loved him with an everlasting love, and technically remained a virgin until my heart, mind, body, soul, and spirit would no longer allow me to remain one. We were both eighteen years old and made an adult decision.

During our senior year, a lot happened. For one, Hotchkiss hosted a dance in which there a bump contest. Everyone knew how to bump, and you had to bump skillfully with your partner, allowing only your hip to gently tap your partner's hip. In a dance contest, one must be creative with making moves that are original and that no one else has the courage to do. That describes the way we danced with each other that night while bumping. We became one of three couples in the finals. I wore a white turtleneck and black and white plaid baggy pants.

Kabrian and I danced the night away. We bumped every way we could imagine, including some bumps that were provocative. The crowd loved it, and since their applause chose the winner, we won. We perspired like crazy, and we were so pleased with our joint effort. The grand prize was a white Hotchkiss coffee mug.

There were no homecoming dances or proms, but at each dance Kabrian and I attended together, I felt as if I were the belle of the ball because of how he treated me. His gentle way made my skin tingle with affection, and I fancied our thoughtful and humorous talks while we slow danced. He was quite the conversationalist, and our discussions made me think deeply. I admired that, because his ideas gave me a different perspective, even if I didn't agree with him.

"Lady Marmalade" by LaBelle and "Midnight Train to Georgia" by Gladys Knight and the Pips were our favorite songs, and as we danced, we sang them to each other. He especially liked the French chorus to "Lady Marmalade". And although both of us took French, we never bothered to use French in our conversations with each other.

One weekend, as I was accompanying Kabrian and his ice hockey team on a bus to a game, he asked, "What would you say if I asked you to marry me?" Most high school girls would have been giddy and gladly said what he wanted to hear, but not me. I was surprised, but not stunned. For over a year, he had given me his devoted attention outside of ice hockey and school. In my heart, I knew how he felt about me, and I felt the same way about him. The only difference was that I wanted more as a young woman in terms of education before I made such a grand commitment. I was not prepared to be a wife, especially a college wife. I wanted to be a college student and knew that I could wait on the Mrs. degree. I didn't want to have to care for anyone but myself during my college years. I wanted to study and learn more and being someone's wife would interfere with my learning and personal achievement. I couldn't have that, at least not at that time.

I replied, "I would say no because I want to go to college." He sank back in his seat. I didn't think anything of his question, because for me it was a no-brainer. I just couldn't imagine going to college as a married woman, and I couldn't imagine not going to college. Besides, that's what prep school was supposed to do, get me ready for college. That would not be the last time that he asked me that question. The second time I gave him the same answer, so he never asked again. I can only imagine how he felt, but I knew that I had to look out for myself. A continued college relationship would have been ideal, but that was not to be.

Our relationship ended strangely. It wasn't because we no longer cared for each other. It wasn't because we wanted to see other people. It was my fear. At the time, Kabrian liked to smoke pot. I didn't smoke anything at all, not even cigarettes like many of the girls at Walker's. When he came to visit, he smoked pot with some of the other black girls. That was not a problem, either. What became the problem was when he shared with Kim and Lynn that he used angel dust on his pot. Since there was no Internet to research "angel dust," I had to rely on my friends' words and worldly knowledge for what "angel dust" was and how it was used recreationally. That scared the hell out of me! I broke it off because of my fear of the effects of angel dust on marijuana on him and how that could impact my life. I was afraid of drug use of any kind.

The days and weeks that followed proved to be difficult. I longed for his letters, attention, and affection, but I had to remind myself continuously why I had been so clear with him, but most importantly, honest with myself. It wasn't a perfect relationship, but it certainly was a good one. It was good because I had learned how to love someone who dared to allow me to be myself. It was good because he loved me and showed his love in numerous ways. I had never had that before from a young man. The kicker was that I was not mature enough to enter a marriage relationship or understanding enough to try to work through his recreational drug use. And since the drugs were illegal, I couldn't discuss the situation with any adult at Walker's or at home. I did what I knew to do relying on my not-yet-fully-developed teen brain. I longed for a different outcome, but there was none. We parted ways without any harsh feelings. He was hurt, but he knew I loved him. I knew I loved myself even more.

38

Tonsillitis

Each Thanksgiving break was spent with my sister, LaWanda, at her place on Staten Island. Initially, I rode the bus or train from Connecticut to the Port Authority bus station in Manhattan and waited for her to pick me up. I was clueless as to the journey she took to get me. All I knew was that I waited for hours in a strange place with even stranger people.

Going up the escalator for the first time at that bus station, I noticed a man clothed in a garment that draped his body. It was like a toga folded and pinned in several places for it to stay intact on his body. What startled me though was his haircut. He was bald all over except for a square-inch patch of blonde hair that looked like a small ponytail. A barrette clamped it in place. I learned that he was a representative of Hari Krishna and passed out brochures as he recruited others to become believers of his way to God. He didn't bother me. As a newcomer to the city, I had no idea what that meant and would have had no response to his efforts. In Pine Bluff, there were Baptists,

Methodists, and Catholics. That was it, so seeing someone of a different faith dressed so differently was foreign.

Wanda told me to wait for her at the information booth. She warned me against talking to strangers, and said if I had a question, to talk only to the people in the information booth. She said if a male person tried to pick me up, tell a police officer or get help in the booth.

I waited for what seemed like an eternity that first time, not realizing the distance Wanda had to travel. As a teen, I had no real appreciation for her effort and commitment to take good care of me. She did way more than most big sisters would do, and I learned how to appreciate all that she did to help make my Walker's experience easier.

As a new traveler, I packed too much for a weekend trip, but the suitcases came in handy as a seat while I waited. We went through this routine a few times until I got the hang of traveling in the City. Thanksgiving break of my junior year was complicated.

Clear signs that I was not feeling well were my loss of my appetite and lack of conversation. That Thanksgiving, I came down with an extremely sore throat, the kind of sore throat where you don't want to swallow your own spit because of the pain. I was miserable, and I held my spit in my mouth until I could no longer afford to not swallow it and had to spit.

The pain was unbearable, and I shed silent tears with each swallow. If I was outside, I spat on the street or grass with a thick trail of spittle. With each swallow or spitting, I wanted to cry aloud because of the agony. My condition made enjoying Thanksgiving dinner a tremendous challenge. Although Wanda prepared a feast for me and her boyfriend, I only nibbled at parts of the soft foods so my throat wouldn't hurt as much. She offered to take me to a doctor, but I said I would wait until I got back to school to see the infirmary doctor.

Stores in New York City were known for the big shopping deals the day after Thanksgiving. Everyone looked for bargains at Macy's and Gimble's. Wanda wanted to go shopping that day, and I wanted to go, too, even with a sore throat. As we left her apartment, it began to rain. It was a misty cold rain, the kind that chills you, even though you're not very wet. The weather conditions did not help my illness, but we shopped anyway.

I don't remember anything that we bought, but I remember how miserable I was the entire time. Once we left Staten Island, there was no turning back, so I suffered willingly through the entire day. The only thing I could do for the rest of the weekend was rest.

The train ride back to Walker's was an adventure. They oversold the tickets, and prep school and college students filled the train cars. By the time I boarded the train, there were no seats anywhere and not even standing room. No one could stand in the aisles. A friend and I ended up riding in the breezeway between two train cars, sitting on our suitcases. We were in a dangerous spot, but we made it.

My first stop on Monday morning was to see Dr. Weipert. He took one look at my throat and told me that my enlarged tonsils were causing the pain. They were in bad shape with holes in them. He gave me an antibiotic and admitted me to the infirmary for a few days until I was fever free. Gradually, I was able to eat solid foods again, and Dr. Weipert released me from the infirmary. The pain subsided, and my tonsils were not as swollen.

That Christmas vacation, I went to see my pediatrician, Dr. Townsend. He said my tonsils would have to be removed. I told him that I went to school in Connecticut and asked if we could wait until spring break or the summer. He said waiting until the summer would probably be best and would give me adequate recovery time. Dr. Townsend also diagnosed me with a heart murmur and gave me pills to take. He said I could continue my regular activities, but that I would need to take an antibiotic before having any dental work. The surgery was scheduled for June 11th, two days after I was scheduled to be home from Walker's. It would be a two-night stay at Jefferson Hospital. That's how I ended up having a tonsillectomy at seventeen.

39

Hester Prynne, *Hamlet* and the Holocaust

Junior year at Walker's was a time of tremendous personal and academic growth for me. I began to learn in a new and different way. I was settling into the environment and had learned more about classroom expectations. As I relaxed, I began to be more vocal in my classes, especially my English classes.

Eleventh grade English consisted of reading more of the classics, especially American literature, and included exercises in strengthening our vocabulary. Teachers included vocabulary and grammar lessons in preparation for the standardized tests. The clear expectation was that we would strive to do our best on those tests and in our class work in hopes of getting into a good college.

Two teachers taught junior English that year. One was a new teacher to Walker's and the other teacher had a reputation for being hard. Mrs. Georgia Lawson insisted we learn vocabulary words each week, and she quizzed us on them. She also required we memorize and recite in front of the class a number of lines from *Hamlet* and *Macbeth*. I was fascinated most, however, by our reading of *The Scarlet Letter*.

From the beginning of Hawthorne's work, I was intrigued by the story. I thought about how bold Hester Prynne had to be in carrying a baby publicly. I also thought about how unfortunate it was for her to bear the burden of parenting alone and to endure the shame and ridicule for what she had done with a man. There was no justice for Hester Prynne. In some ways, it reminded me of my own family situation. My *Scarlet Letter* paper was one of the best papers that I wrote while at Walker's. Perhaps it was the subject matter and the connections I made to the characters. The book, theme, and characters held meaning for me unlike many of the other books we read.

I studied the Holocaust and its impact on Jewish people. Mrs. Lawson encouraged us to read about it, and we watched films of the destruction of human bodies. Most memorable for me was the film chronicling a tractor moving skulls, bones, and ashes of Jewish people. It was as if their lives had no value. While I understood many of the atrocities of American slavery, I did not understand white-on-white genocide. It took the explanations of my history teacher to help me understand what the Holocaust was about and why that happened to European Jewish people. The persecutions they endured simply because of their heritage reminded me so clearly of the persecutions people of color experience. Black Americans had done nothing to anyone to be treated in the ways they were treated in America. I began to make connections from the Holocaust to what was happening to us, to me, to my people.

In coming to terms with what I was learning and what I witnessed in my world, our pop culture addressed the societal ills we faced. A series of *Blaxploitation* movies like *Super Fly*, *Foxy Brown*, *Coffy*, *Claudine*, and *Shaft* portrayed life in America for urban blacks. And all that the images on the movie screens did not get across to viewers, the lyrics of the musical scores did. They showed us ourselves. And although I did not come from a city with urban problems, similar problems pervaded rural communities and small towns in the South.

The musical genius of Curtis Mayfield set our world ablaze with captivating lyrics from the *Super Fly* soundtrack. His words made us think clearly about the plight of those living in urban decay in America's inner cities, a different kind of holocaust as the lives of thousands of black and brown Americans were wasted through drug use and abuse and all sorts of violent acts often not of their own choosing, but of a carefully and intentionally orchestrated system of genocide designed solely for those living in American urban poor communities. It was America's unidentified and unspoken holocaust. And although the Jewish Holocaust in Europe ended many years ago, the American holocaust designed for the denigration and genocide of urban black, brown, and poor people has yet to end.

I discovered that holocausts come in many forms. Sometimes it's the holocaust of the mind that causes the most damage to humans, that constant and nagging message that you're not good enough no matter how well you do or the effort that you put forth. It's the constant reminder that although you had nothing to do with your parentage or your birth, you must pay the price for being who you are. It's the ceaseless mind holocaust that focuses on the destruction of the spirit as well as the body. And, yes, it is also the persistent destruction of black, brown, and poor bodies that makes America's unspoken holocaust so virulent and catastrophic for those who live and die in it.

Our concern, frustration and surprise in this country only come when the victims are white. In America, change will come to our holocaust when the victims are not urban, black, brown, or poor.

***

I was scheduled to fly home on the Saturday before Walker's commencement. Somehow my wires were crossed, and I missed my flight. Mrs. West worked with the airline and was able to get me on a flight out of Hartford the following Monday morning. That meant I was around for Anne and Mary's graduation. It gave me a chance to see a Walker's commencement. Jimmie, on the other hand, was a bit concerned because my surgery was the following Tuesday, and I had to be home in time for that.

I stayed for the graduation ceremony, and Miss Sue agreed to chaperone me and get me to the airport on Monday. The dorms closed after commencement ended, which meant that I had to stay in her apartment that night. After graduation, she asked me if I had ever seen the ocean or been to a beach. When I said no, she said we would take a car trip to the beach in Rhode Island.

On the way to the beach, we stopped in a town with a couple of stores that Miss Sue liked. One was an Izod Lacoste store, and there I saw the accessories that the wealthy girls wore with their uniforms and the clothes that their parents wore. We went to a Lily store and found another sampling of the colorful clothes others at Walker's wore. While colorful, those clothes never appealed to me as something that was representative of who I was or who I wanted to become. They were pretty frocks, but not anything in which I would feel comfortable. Miss Sue bought some accessories from each store, and we headed to the beach.

We passed Mystic Seaport in New London, Connecticut and the naval base. In the port was a huge military vessel that was probably an aircraft carrier. It was a vast military greenish-gray ship with huge white letters printed on the side. It carried soldiers and military equipment. I stared at it out the rearview mirror until it was out of sight. I had never seen anything that big on water.

Our trip to the beach was an amazing outing. What an ocean view! There was water as far as I could see, and the water was so vast as it met the horizon. I had never been on a beach before and had certainly not seen that much water. I wondered what lay beyond the edge of the water.

I eagerly removed my shoes and socks and walked out on the sand. I had images from television of what one does on the beach. The Coppertone commercials for suntan lotion showed little white kids having a great time running about and building sandcastles. I decided to look for seashells and build a sandcastle. No one told me that I needed beach-going equipment such as a pail and shovel to complete either task, but I went looking for shells anyway and attempted to build a sandcastle with my bare hands. While I found a few shells, the sandcastle did not happen. It was just a mound of sand.

After getting our feet wet and sand between our toes, we ate at a seafood shack on the beach. For the first time, I ate oysters, both steamed and raw. I still remember grinding the grittiness of the raw oysters with the sand still inside them. Miss Sue assured me that was normal for fresh oysters right out of the water. I tried them, but they were not appetizing.

We drove back to Walker's that night, and I slept on her couch. Her dog slept in her bedroom with the door closed. The next morning, we went to the airport in Hartford, and I flew home. My tonsillectomy was the next day.

40

Summer Ease

My recovery from my tonsillectomy was painful. Although I was promised lots of Jell-O and ice cream, I wanted neither because my throat remained sore after the surgery. I just sat in the hospital bed holding spittle in my mouth, trying not to swallow, and trying not to cry. The doctor and nurse assured me that it would get better if I just swallowed instead of holding my spit in my mouth. I didn't believe them, and it took more than a day for them to convince me to swallow. Jimmie told me that crying would make the pain worse.

Our family has always been one to take extra precautions when it comes to health and wellness. If it was not necessary for us to go out in inclement weather, we didn't. If someone had surgery of any kind, the expectation was that you remained in the house for several days or weeks after the surgery to recover just to be on the safe side. My tonsillectomy was no different. I am sure they took these precautions because of the poor healthcare blacks traditionally received in their lifetime, and they wanted to do whatever they could to ensure my wellbeing. By the time my family considered me healed and able to get out of the house, the Fourth of July was nearing. Before I left Walker's in June, I signed up to take the SAT and the Achievement tests again at Central High School in mid-July. I took the tests on two different Saturday mornings knowing that my scores would arrive right before it was time for me to return to Walker's in late August.

Pine Bluff public schools dismissed for the summer in May, and all graduations occurred before the end of May. By the time I arrived home, the local students already had summer jobs. The best I could hope for was babysitting for families who knew me. I had babysitting experience from sitting for LaWanda's friend Ruth who had a pre-teen daughter named Tammie. Occasionally, when I visited Wanda, Ruth would ask me to keep Tammie while she worked. Tammie went to a Catholic school, and frequently, she had breaks at the same time I had breaks from Walker's. I babysat for a few weeks in Pine Bluff for a family I had known all my life. Their sweet baby girl was quiet and playful. She enjoyed food and took long naps. It was an ideal babysitting job. Her parents picked me up and returned me to my house at the end of the day. It wasn't much money, but it gave me pocket change to buy snacks and sweet treats.

The summer between my junior and senior years was uneventful. While recuperating from my surgery, I wrote letters to Nyoka, Kim, and Lynn. I let them know how I was doing and kept them abreast of my summer activities. They wrote back, and we exchanged letters throughout the summer months.

Anna Karenina was on the reading list that summer, and by the time I got into reading it, it was time to return to

Walker's. There were two additional books, but those titles escape me. There was no consideration for student choice or voice regarding literature. The adults decided which books would be appropriate for teen girls to read and which ones would be most helpful to us in our growth and development. All of us read the same books and were tested on them in some way by the teachers when we returned. It was more stories about white people. It was as if we needed to learn about the ways and struggles of whites, but there was never any need to learn about the lives and struggles of black people. Perhaps had we read books by black writers, we could have had meaningful dialogues about all of our lives in America. And although Ralph Ellison, James Baldwin, Alice Walker, Zora Neale Hurston, Toni Morrison, Paul Laurence Dunbar, Maya Angelou, Claude McCay, Sterling Brown, Gwendolyn Brooks, Nikki Giovanni, Langston Hughes, Lorraine Hansberry, and others were prolific black writers, not one time was a title by an author of color ever mentioned as an option. No one was looking out for our interests. There was no watchman.

41

Collision Course

When I left home for Walker's, our family had only had a car for about three years, so learning to drive was not a priority. I did not dream of taking the car out for a spin, or even of running errands. I was fine walking to the store to pick up a few items.

At Walker's, however, getting a driver's license was important. Although only one student had a car on campus, many girls took driver's education during junior year. Girls sixteen years old and older took the class. Like my classmates, I eagerly signed up for the class and for the on-the-road lessons. We had several in-class lectures from a Connecticut State Police officer. He showed us films of horrific car accidents in which teens had died. Those films were supposed to scare us into following all traffic rules when driving. No drinking and driving and no speeding. Keep your eyes and mind on the road. Keep your hands at ten and two.

In addition to the classes, we had actual driving lessons on the Simsbury and surrounding area roads. My first driving lesson was supposed to occur the day after a heavy Connecticut snow. I assumed they would reschedule my lesson, so I did not leave my room at Cluett to meet the state trooper at Beaverbrook. Whenever it snowed in Arkansas, no one drove anywhere. Safety officials always advised us to stay home and off the roads.

The telephone on my hall rang. A knock on my door let me know I had a call.

"Hello," I said. It was Mrs. West.

"Veda, did you know you have a driving lesson today?"

"Yes, but I thought it would be rescheduled because of the snow."

"Well, it wasn't. The state trooper is here for your lesson."

"I've never driven, let alone driven on snow and ice."

"Well, you'd better get on down here. He's waiting. And we've already paid for your lessons." She sounded like a mother.

Reluctantly, I put on my boots, coat, hat, and gloves, and trudged down the hill to Beaverbrook. There, waiting in the lobby, was the state trooper in his official uniform and hat.

"Hi, I'm Veda. I just thought you would reschedule my lesson because of the snow. Where I'm from, no one drives on snow and ice."

"Where's that?"

"Arkansas." It seemed as if I was always explaining something about Arkansas.

"Well, in Connecticut, everyone drives on snow and ice. This will be a good lesson for you. Let's go."

We headed out the front door. Once in the car, he watched to make sure that I completed tasks like adjusting the mirrors and the driver's seat and buckling my seatbelt. He told me to drive around the circle and head up the road to Cluett. What he didn't know was that while the road leading to the dorm was clear, not all the area around the dorm was cleared. I drove slowly up the road, being careful to avoid girls walking towards me on the left and the trees on the right. As we neared the dorm, he instructed me to go behind the dorm and turn around. Why did he do that?

Behind Cluett that day was the thickest sheet of ice and snow I had ever seen. I knew I was in for a world of trouble. Who has her first driving lesson on a thick sheet of ice? I turned the car onto the sheet of ice and snow. The state trooper told me to back out and turn around to go back in the direction of Beaverbrook. That sounded reasonable, but it became a challenging driving task.

"First, put the car in reverse. Then, turn the steering wheel completely to the right before you give it any gas," he directed me.

I did exactly as he said.

"Now, give it some gas. Not too much, just enough to get the car moving."

I did that, too, but what resulted was not what either of us expected. The car was stuck on the ice and snow, and the wheels just spun. No movement, just burning rubber on the ice. I looked at him for more directions.

"What should I do?"

"Let's try it again. Start over."

Again, I put the car in drive and then again in reverse. I turned the wheels to the right and gave it some gas again. Spinning and more spinning. After the third and fourth tries, I hoped the state trooper would come to my aid, excuse me from the driver's seat, and take over driving, but he did not. I was on my own. Since the car was designed for driver's education lessons, the state trooper had a set of gears on his side of the car as well as a brake to stop the car.

He used none of those gears nor the brake. I struggled on that snow and ice for at least twenty minutes. Girls began looking out of second floor windows wondering who was behind the wheel of a state police car stuck on ice. Thankfully, they couldn't see me, but word traveled down the hill to Beaverbrook that someone was stuck on ice at Cluett. By a process of elimination, everyone found out it was me. I spent twenty minutes of a thirty-minute driving lesson slipping and sliding on snow and ice.

Eventually, the state trooper changed course and told me how to turn in the direction of the skid to get off of the ice. We made small movements back and forth that eventually inched the vehicle out of the icy rut I made burning rubber with the wheels. By the time we got from behind Cluett, I was a nervous wreck and wondered if I would ever have another driving lesson in Connecticut weather.

The state trooper helped me learn to listen differently for instructions and how to follow them from a more capable driver. I had one vision of the driving lesson, but he had another. I thought the lesson would be easy and follow the path of things most familiar to me. He had a vision that included learning how to live and drive in adverse road conditions. His goal was to teach me how to survive in the driver's seat no matter where I was. He was intentional about his goals for me as a student learning how to drive for the first time, and he persisted.

I learned an important life lesson. I realized that even in adverse situations, like driving for the first time on snow and ice, I can come through them successfully if I focus and put the right effort and energy in the right places at the right time. I learned that with the right teacher, anything is possible. I discovered it's necessary to take precautions when learning something new, and it's essential to listen to the teacher. I had to listen with both my ears and my heart.

***

Summers in Pine Bluff are brutally hot and humid for days on end. With temperatures hovering near 100 degrees, no one wants to go outside in the heat. If you have a car, driving is the preferred means of transportation, but cars get hot too.

I completed the driver's education course with the help of the state trooper. When I presented my certificate of completion to Jimmie the following summer, it held no weight. I could not drive at home until I passed the written and road tests in Arkansas. The written test was easy for me, and I passed on the first try. I also quickly took and passed the road test that included parallel parking. Still Jimmie was reluctant to let me drive with or without her. I was seventeen years old, and in Arkansas teens can drive alone at sixteen. It was weeks that summer before she allowed me to drive by myself. Meanwhile, Buster drove at fifteen without the benefit of driver's education or having passed either the written or the road test. Go figure.

It was that summer that my worlds collided. The Connecticut state trooper taught me to check my mirrors before putting the car in gear so I could see around the entire car. He scored me on that detail in my final road lesson. When I got home for the summer, I attempted to continue his instructions. In my mind, he was the authority on driving. Jimmie told me to leave her mirrors alone. Being who I was, I explained what the state trooper taught me. She made it clear to me she didn't care what he'd said. She wanted me to keep my hands off her mirrors.

There was no carport or garage, so the car sat on a slab of concrete in our driveway. One day someone forgot to leave the windows cracked for cool air to circulate, so the car was extremely hot when we got ready to go to the store. I volunteered to drive with Jimmie in the passenger seat. Out of pure habit, I reached to adjust the rear-view mirror, and it came off the windshield into my hand. The adhesive holding it in place had softened with the heat. I tried to put it back, but it wouldn't stay. Jimmie looked at me, said a few choice words, and gave me a backhand hit. I cried the ugly cry. It was strange how learning to drive caused such conflict. I wanted to follow the directions I'd learned in driver's education, but it was more important for me to follow my mother's directions. I wanted to do the right thing, but there was no right thing. She drove us to the store.

42

College Applications

She strutted through the Beaverbrook lobby with a long-legged gait that exuded confidence a plenty and a delicate swag, yet she seemed quiet and reserved. With every smooth step, she made each hallway a runway. She owned every step of her stride, and we knew it. Bonnie MacDougall, a nice white lady, came to Walker's my junior year. She was an English teacher, who taught mostly seniors in courses like A Survey of Shakespeare and British Literature. I wanted to get to know her, so I took her Shakespeare course. Somehow, she was able to infuse energy into the Bard's work, which made it engaging and enlightening at the same time. When we had an aha moment with a passage, her mouth turned up at the corners, and she broke into a smile that said, "Yes, you got it." Miss MacDougall always had a kind word for her students and found humor in everyday learning and living. She was young, and her insights were a breath of fresh air.

Often, we acted out scenes from the plays. As a newbie to the works of Shakespeare beyond *Hamlet*, I was unfamiliar with several quotes. Of note was a scene at the end of *Julius Caesar*. One day, as I read the lines with a partner and added my own dramatics to the play, I read my last line incorrectly. I played Caesar and another classmate played Brutus. As Caesar recognizes his betrayal and that his protégé, Brutus, is part of his assassination, Caesar says, "Et tu, Brute?" I read the lines just as I thought the words were pronounced with "Brute" pronounced as one syllable, and I dramatically fell to the floor in death. The class erupted with laughter. At first, I thought the class was laughing at my theatrics. I later learned that, in that scene, "Brute" was pronounced as two syllables with an emphasis on the last one. I had never heard that line. Instead of taking offense at their laughter, I joined their laughter and proudly took a bow.

For a few days after that incident, my classmates said the line whenever they saw me in the hallway, the dorm or in the dining hall. I continued to share a laugh with them. Perhaps I should have been offended by their laughter, but I took it lightly. I still had a lot to learn, and I was okay with a little self-deprecating humor.

Learning Shakespeare was just one of the things I learned from Miss MacDougall. As it turned out, she would be influential in my college decision. In an informal conversation one day, she asked me where I was thinking of applying to college. I told her I really wanted to go to Mt. Holyoke, but that I was applying to other schools as safety schools like the University of Arkansas at Fayetteville and Briarcliff College in New York, just in case admission to Mt. Holyoke didn't happen.

"Hmmm. Those sound like interesting places," she said. "But have you considered some other places?

"Not really."

"Who's your advisor?"

"Mrs. Huntington. I've had her for about a year."

"Have you talked about your college applications?"

"A little bit. She just told me to let her know how she can help. We really didn't talk about where I would apply and which colleges would be best for me. Marion thinks I should apply to Princeton, but I'm not so sure I can get in."

"Who is Marion? And what does he know about Princeton?"

"He's my older cousin, but I call him my brother. He went to Exeter, then to Princeton."

"Okay. That's good to know. He may have some connections that can help you get into Princeton. So, here's what I think. You should think about what you want to do and then think about where you might want to go to school. Princeton is a great school."

"I've known since I was in third grade that I want to major in English. Lots of places have English programs."

"Yes, they do. What do you want to do with an English major?"

"I think I want to work for a publisher in New York after college. I don't know how all that works, but that's what I want to do. I like writing, and I think I'm good at it."

"Yes, you are a very good writer. Have you considered Wesleyan University? It's in Middletown, not too far from here. They have a great English department with distinguished professors."

"No, I haven't. Is it hard to get into?" I needed to know more. She had piqued my curiosity in ways that no one else had. Miss MacDougall was willing to have a thoughtful conversation with me about going to college.

"It can be. It's one of the Little Three with Williams College and Amherst. I think you should give it a shot."

"If you think so. No one else has mentioned it to me. I think Emily Peterson, who graduated last year, goes there. But what about Mt. Holyoke?

"What's so special about Mt. Holyoke?"

"Well, it's one of the Seven Sisters, and it's all female."

"Do you still want to go to school with all females?"

"Not really, but I'm really afraid of going to a big school with males and females after being here."

"You'll be fine in a co-ed school. And Wesleyan is not that big. I think they have about 2,000 students."

"Compared to Walker's, that's huge."

"I know, but most colleges have a lot more than that. That's considered a small college."

"Okay, I'll write and request an application."

"Oh, by the way, how are your SAT scores?"

"They're pretty good."

"Did you break a thousand in English and math combined?"

"Yes, I did."

"You will be fine, then. Wesleyan is considered a highly selective college, so they will be looking carefully at your test scores and teacher recommendations."

And that's how my first college application conference went. It was a one-shot conversation with Miss MacDougall. From that point on, she became my advisor for my college application process. She seemed to know the most about applying to college and to take the most interest in me and my efforts. As I prepared my applications and my essays, I took them to her for a review. She gave me feedback that helped me accurately and succinctly respond to the questions. Her edits seemed reasonable and helped me polish my essays into pieces that would make admission committees curious about me as a candidate and potential student.

All my college applications were completed before the Christmas vacation from Walker's. Miss MacDougall wrote my English teacher letter of recommendation, and I had Mrs. Huntington write my other letter. There was no way my math teacher could or would have given me a good recommendation, even though my grades in Algebra II with her were a lot better than my geometry grades. Before Christmas, Walker's allowed us to sit for the SAT one last time just to boost our scores. My scores inched up another notch, and I applied to Wesleyan and the other schools.

Finally, here was someone at Walker's who thought I had lots of potential and something to offer. The thought drew a toothy grin across my face, and I began to believe in me again.

***

Miss MacDougall didn't know the true impact she had on my life. Her influence was positive and helped me grow because I processed the words I heard about myself as positives instead of negatives. As I thought about myself, her comments were insightful and helped me see more of who I was and could become. I took her care, concern, and comments as tools I could use in making decisions about college. While I didn't know where any of her thoughts and ideas would lead me, I was willing to trust the process and try.

43

In the Bottle

Growing up in our home in Pine Bluff, drinking alcohol of any kind was taboo. No beer, no wine, no whiskey. Nothing. Drinking was a sin before God. I did not know how to drink, let alone what to drink. Jimmie and Dollee put the fear of God in me about drinking, and most of my friends did not drink alcohol when I left Pine Bluff. I was frightened even more when I saw a Walker's student vomit for hours one night after having had too much to drink. She emptied the contents of her stomach, mostly alcohol and milk chocolate, on the carpeted floors of Cluett. The stench of her puke remained in my smell sensitive nostrils for a long time, and I will never forget her pale white skin, her bulging green eyes, and her slimy hands as she knelt on the floor trying to rid her system of the poison she had imbibed. I knew I did not want that to be my experience.

Gil Scott-Heron expressed fear and trepidation over the power of alcohol and alcoholism in the lives of black, brown and poor folks living in urban ghettos in his 1970's song, "In the Bottle." His lyrics called us to think about the plight of those who drink alcohol to forget their life's woes. He sang of men and women who had time after time forfeited personal possessions, jobs, and relationships just to hold on to their alcohol bottles.

Jimmie and Dollee warned my siblings and me against alcohol use. For them, drinking alcohol of any kind was a sin before God that could and would destroy our lives and everything we worked to achieve. As a child and young adult, I believed almost everything they told me. For example, I never watched television while it was thundering and lightning for fear of being struck by lightning. They told me that was dangerous, so I listened. The only rebellious part of me was my mouth.

In December of my senior year, I turned eighteen and had never had a drink of alcohol. One year, Buster and I used Mogen David blackberry wine to spike the iced tea for Marion's friends who came to dinner. Dollee's physician prescribed drinking that wine to improve her iron levels. Buster and I thought it would be a good idea to put some in the tea. It only made the tea taste sour. No one even got a buzz.

The only other time I had tasted alcohol was in the annual Christmas fruitcakes Dollee made. Cautiously, she brought home a carefully measured single cup of clear alcohol in a Mason jar from her job and dared us to touch it. I never did. I was always afraid of the consequences, perceived or real.

"So, Veda, what are you going to do for your eighteenth birthday?" Miss Sue asked.

"Nothing special. It's right before finals, and I have papers to write."

"Hmmm? You're turning eighteen, and don't have any plans?"

"No, I don't. Where would I go, and what would I do?

"We'll think of something."

"All right, but I still have to write my papers."

"Why don't you and the others come over to my place after dinner on your birthday?" She meant the other black girls.

"I can come, and I'll see what the other girls are doing."

"Can you come about 7 p.m.?"

"I guess so. Somebody may have study hall, but I'll see who can come."

On December 6th, we trudged across the road to the pink brick building where some of Walker's faculty lived. Miss Sue lived in one of the one-bedroom apartments. Nyoka, Lynn, and Kim joined me. Upon our arrival, her dog greeted us with a hearty bark. I shook for a second, then remembered that the dog would settle down and be gentle once we got inside.

Miss Sue had a small kitchenette, a breakfast bar, and two barstools. It was just enough room for her to cook a small meal on her pint-sized stove. On the bar, Miss Sue had prepared our activity for the evening. I would be introduced to alcohol for the first time.

"Veda, I have some alcohol here I thought you might like to try. Have you ever tried beer or a mixed drink?"

"No," I said hesitantly. I knew I was of age to partake. At that time, the legal drinking age in Connecticut was eighteen. I knew I could buy cigarettes and alcohol. What I didn't know was how the alcohol would taste or make me feel. I was properly warned about getting drunk, and I didn't want that to happen to me. Drinking alcohol on campus was against the school rules. I guess technically we weren't on the school grounds, but in a teacher's apartment. What was this teacher doing? She was aiding and abetting a willful violation of the school's honor code.

"Will I get drunk?" I wanted to know.

"Probably not from this amount. If you drink too much, you might feel a buzz," Miss Sue said.

"Come on, Vee. Try it," Nyoka encouraged me. "You won't get drunk. I'll see to that." She was always looking out for me.

"Have you had alcohol before?" Miss Sue asked Nyoka directly.

"What kind of question is that?" Nyoka clapped back.

"You have? What about the rest of you?"

They all nodded yes. I just sat there, wondering how they could have had access to alcohol as kids.

Here I was, the oldest one in the group, with the least amount of experience with alcohol. I wasn't surprised about Nyoka, but I thought the others were too young to even have experimented with alcohol. Nyoka told me that she had plenty of experience with alcohol. Her favorite drink was rum and coke. She had even been to a nightclub. We had lived truly different lives, and here we were at the same place.

Miss Sue first poured me a beer. It fizzed in my mouth, and it wasn't sweet. Suds covered my top lip, and I reached for a napkin to remove the evidence. The other girls giggled. Next, she poured a cup of red wine.

"What's the difference in the wines?"

"You can learn about that later. I just want you to taste each drink so you will know if you like it or not. Don't worry, I'm not going to let you get drunk."

I took a sip of the wine. It tasted strong and not like the grape juice I had imagined it would. The sting of the alcohol stunned me, and I wanted to spit it out, but as the oldest, I couldn't be the chicken. While I was sampling the different adult beverages, Nyoka, Lynn, and Kim drank what I left in the glasses. And as they swallowed the alcohol, Miss Sue poured more so everyone could have a nice swig.

Since Nyoka told me that she liked rum and coke, I asked if I could taste that, too. Miss Sue mixed the drink and handed it to me. When I took a big gulp, Nyoka told me to slow down and drink it slowly. She said that's how people get drunk. I was just anxious to taste the sweetness of the coke, and I wasn't thinking about the effects of the rum. I put down the drink, and Nyoka finished it.

That night, I tasted wine, beer, and whiskey. Each time, I either sipped or dipped my tongue into the alcohol, I still heard Jimmie's admonitions and feared the possibility of getting drunk. Nobody had ever told me how much I'd have to drink to get drunk.

I did not get drunk that night, and I didn't even get a buzz. Neither did any of the other girls. We never told anyone at Walker's about that night, and we never discussed it. That was our little secret.

44

Reparations

*"*H*ark the herald angels shout, twenty more days till we get out. No more books and no more thinking. Lots of sex, dope, and drinking. One more chorus for the road, I'm as horny as a toad. Hark the herald angels shout; twenty more days till we get out."*

Those were the words that seniors at Cluett sang to the tune of "Hark the Herald Angels Sing" as we stood on the balcony each night leading up to our Christmas vacation. The chorus started on the first night back from Thanksgiving break, and every night was a countdown. The singing went on even in frigid temperatures and on snowy nights. I joined the group in singing this little ditty most nights. Nyoka never did. She thought it was much too silly and simple for high school girls, especially seniors. For me, it was a welcomed break, however brief, from reading, writing papers, and studying for finals.

Before our Christmas vacation, Walker's decided to hold a slave auction as a fundraiser for some worthy cause. The development office hosted the fundraiser, and the teachers and administrators volunteered to participate as slaves. As black students, we never considered the undertones or the overtones of having such an event at the school. For us, there was no connection to slavery in America and this event. What were we thinking? And there was no guidance from a more capable adult to help us process the racism inherent in this activity. We were just eager to participate with the few coins that we had.

On the day of the auction, we decided to pool our funds to buy a teacher. We tossed around several names of teachers we would like to buy. Instantly, I knew whom we should buy, but I had to have agreement from the other girls to get the teacher whom I wanted to get. The person whose services we would purchase had to do whatever within reason the slave owner wanted done, and that included cleaning.

I wanted to buy Miss Tregillus. As the other girls talked about other teachers, I yelled out Ms. Tregillus. Robin and Nyoka had had their own run-ins with her in math class, too. She had suspected them of cheating and made them re-take a test. Both made A's on the re-take, but that experience left a distaste for her. We agreed as a group to buy Miss Tregillus for my personal use.

What we didn't know as we decided to pool our money was that there were other girls who disliked her, just as much as we did, and they wanted to buy her, also. I never knew what their stories were, but there was a lot of interest in buying her services.

As the auction proceeded, we agreed I would take the lead in bidding on Miss Tregillus. Other teachers and administrators were bought and sold for small sums, including the headmaster, Mr. Pierce. Miss Tregillus was another story. I was outbid repeatedly. It became apparent that other girls wanted to get back at her, as well, but they all knew about how she had treated me in geometry and remembered watching my discomfort. At some point in the auction, the other girls ceased bidding and gave me their money so I could win the bid on getting Miss Tregillus. I ended up with the winning bid, and she was mine to do whatever I wanted her to do for an afternoon.

"Woohoo!" I yelled and slapped a high five with the other black girls.

There was sheer jubilation. We cheered and danced a little jig, and the other girls joined in our excitement with laughter.

"What are you going to do with her?" Kim asked.

"Are you going to make her do dirty work?" Lynn inquired.

"Vee, just be nice," Nyoka admonished. "Don't let her change who you are."

"Okay. I'm thinking. I'm thinking," was my only response.

Being the meticulous person that she was about work, time, and scheduling, Miss Tregillus immediately came to me and asked when she should report to do her work. We agreed on a date and time. She would come the day before I would leave for Arkansas for the break.

Miss Tregillus arrived at my room in Cluett at the appointed time. Nyoka and I had several conversations about what her tasks would be for the time that I had her. We were finishing finals and getting ready to leave campus for the Christmas vacation. I had been busy writing papers and making sure I had completed and submitted my college applications. I had even done my laundry. I had not had time to clean my room and pack my suitcases for the trip home. I would be in Pine Bluff for a month, and I had a lot to pack. Her job that day was packing my clothes and cleaning my room.

While Miss Tregillus was there, I left my room door open so that other students in Cluett who passed by could see her hard at work. Some of them laughed and snickered at seeing her work with me as the "owner" of her body and actions for a short time. I was not mean or disrespectful, and I ended up learning a lot that day from her. Perhaps I was more attentive because it was an informal setting, or maybe it was because *she* had to do what I wanted her to do and not the other way around. Through this process, I found another human being inside of her, who cared for her students, but who didn't know how to show it.

I learned that while stern and strict, there was a gentle soul inside. Her interest in math had made her into an extremely structured and organized person. She saw the world in geometric shapes, and she viewed packing my belongings as a welcome opportunity to solve yet another geometry problem.

During our afternoon together, she asked me questions about my home life and what life was like in Pine Bluff. She had limited family contact, and most of her vacation time was spent at Walker's. I thought what a lonely life that must be.

I also learned from her how to efficiently pack clothing into small spaces. She showed me how to neatly fold my garments and then roll them before placing them in my suitcase. And although she rolled many pieces of my clothing that day, my suitcases were still quite full. She remarked, "You have a lot of things."

When she finished packing, she cleaned my room, dusting and vacuuming the floor. Not once did she shrink back from anything I asked her to do, and not one time did

I treat her like she was less than human. She showed me that she had a heart, and I returned the favor. I treated her with as much dignity and respect as I could muster. I was learning to be a better person to someone who had not always been kind to or supportive of me and my efforts. She was nice to me and showed me that there is dignity in kindness. Although I had purchased her services without her having any say in what she would do that afternoon, she performed every task with pride, grace, and excellence. I couldn't have asked for more. Through that activity, we learned from and about each other in a new and different way. Our respect for each other grew, but I was grateful I would never have her as a teacher again. Thankfully, our paths would only cross outside of a classroom, and that was a good thing. That was my final lesson from Miss Tregillus.

That night, I sang loudly and joyfully with the other girls on the balcony at Cluett.

45

The Interview

"**A**re you going to visit any of the colleges where you applied?" Miss MacDougall asked. While not officially my advisor, she kept watch over my college application process.

"I'm not sure."

"Why not?"

"I guess I'm not sure about going to these places alone and having the money to get there and back."

"Come on, now! You came to Walker's. You can visit those places, too."

"Yes, I guess I could."

"And I am sure Walker's has a fund to help you go. Don't you get college visiting days?"

"Yes, we get three of those, but it would take more than a day for me to visit some of them."

"Yes, it would, but I was thinking about the places that are close by."

"Okay. Those I can think about and check on. Who would I talk to about money to visit these places?"

"Start with Mrs. West. She seems to know how things work around here."

"I'll do that."

I met with Mrs. West one afternoon, and we decided I should visit Briarcliff College. I could take a train in to Westchester County to visit the campus and meet with college personnel. She also said I could use my college visitation days to visit Wesleyan and Mt. Holyoke and that I needed to let her know when I'd like to go for a visit since both were nearby.

On a Monday morning, Mrs. West dropped me off at the Hamden train station for the trip to Briarcliff. It was an uneventful ride. Some folks on the train rode into New York City for work. A gentleman sitting across from me looked up from his newspaper momentarily and asked me where I was going. When I told him, I was going to visit a college, he inquired about my family and why I was going alone. I had never given any thought to having a parent, or anyone else for that matter, accompany me on a college visit. I had not imagined asking Jimmie to go with me. I had come to Walker's all alone, so it just made sense to me that I would take this next step alone as well. From childhood, I had been prepared to move through the world independently, and that day was no different. I told the gentleman that I was going alone and that my family lived in Arkansas. He went back to reading his newspaper.

My visit at the college was not impressive. The campus was gorgeous, but it just seemed like an extension of the life I had at Walker's, and I didn't think that I wanted a similar situation. It was an all-women's college, and although I had some concerns about returning to a co-ed environment, I knew in my heart this college was not the place for me.

After receiving my application for admission, a Wesleyan admissions counselor called. She asked if I wanted to come for an interview. When I told her that I didn't think I could come, she suggested that an alumnus come and interview me at Walker's. Unknown to me, Wesleyan had an interview process whereby a Wesleyan graduate living near the applicant would go, interview the applicant, and submit a written report to the university. I agreed to have the interview.

Victor Anderson, a local white attorney, graduated from Wesleyan when it was still all male. I was one of the first females and the first black applicant he interviewed. He contacted me at Walker's, and we arranged for a day and time to meet. Mr. Anderson arrived on a Thursday night after dinner. We sat facing each other in the powder blue Queen Anne chairs in the Beaverbrook living room.

"Tell me about yourself."

"I'm from Pine Bluff, Arkansas, and this is my third year at Walker's."

"So, how did you get all the way up here from a town in Arkansas?"

"I came here through a program called A Better Chance. They recruit students with good grades and no money to come to places like Ethel Walker. They think these experiences will help give us a better chance in life."

"Does it work?

"I don't know, but I do know that this experience has opened up a whole new world for me."

"How so?"

"Well, first, I've read some books and written some papers I know I wouldn't have written in Pine Bluff."

"How do you know that?

"None of my friends back home have had to do the level of work I have had to do. Sometimes, I've had to read 300 pages a week *and* write papers. I never knew I could stay up all night doing schoolwork, but I have. We even have summer reading, and my friends at home look at me like I'm crazy when I have to go read books over the summer."

"Hmmm? Anything else different?"

"Yes, there are lots of other differences. Not only is the class work different, but they help us get ready for taking tests. You know, tests like the SAT and the Achievement tests. And we all participate in a sport. Last year, our basketball team was undefeated. I was a starter on that team. I have met girls from all over the country and places outside of the U.S. That would not have happened in Pine Bluff."

"Good for you. How has this experience helped you grow?"

"First of all, I've been away from home for three years. I've had to grow up pretty fast and adjust to life away from home. They try to protect us here at Walker's, but you're on your own in the dorms when no one is looking. You have to make grown-up decisions all by yourself. That can be tough when you're a teenager. Sometimes you make the right choices and sometimes you don't."

"I see. That can be difficult sometimes as an adult. At least, for me it can be. So, what has it been like leaving the South and coming here? I've only lived in Connecticut, so I wouldn't know what it's like to live in another place, especially the South."

"Are you asking about prejudice and stuff like that?"

"Yes, if you're okay talking about it."

"For one, it's not really any different living in the South or the North. You always know when people don't like you. You can just feel it. Some people are fake, and others will treat you right."

"How so?"

"In the South, people always tell you when they don't like you. In the North, they don't tell you. They just show you. I'm used to people telling me. Here you sometimes have to guess, and I don't like that."

"What insight! I never thought about prejudice in that way."

The interview was supposed to have lasted for thirty minutes to an hour. We sat and talked for more than two hours. Mr. Anderson took copious notes and used several sheets on his yellow legal pad. During our time together, several girls walked by with inquiring looks, but no one came into the living room. He departed Beaverbrook with lots of information about me, and I still knew little about him. The interview had gone well.

46

The Match

Forgiveness is always a gift when it is received, and no one appreciates it more than the offender. We all like to think of ourselves as being better than we actually are. We excuse our own *faux pas* in hopes that others might not see the not so good qualities that we possess. We have blind spots about who we are and of what we are capable of saying and doing. Truth is, we are all imperfect flesh with human frailties that often manifest at the most inopportune times and hurt others and embarrass us. That was true for me, too. In my heart of hearts, I wanted to believe I always did the right thing. No one can honestly make that claim. We all fail at one juncture or another.

Nyoka and I spent a lot of quality time together. We played tennis when no one else was on the court. It was never a competition, just practice between two friends. She was quick and easy hitting. I moved faster than I ever thought I could and returned fastballs. Sometimes we kept score, and sometimes we didn't. It wasn't important to us.

We wanted to improve. During the winter months, we put on heavy coats and played paddle tennis down by the gym. The grounds crew always cleared the playing surfaces of those courts. When we didn't feel like playing outside at all, we challenged each other to ping pong games in the game room at Cluett. With either game, we enjoyed each other's company until we had more important work to do. She taught me how to cornrow hair and allowed me to practice on her hair. Sometimes, we played two-hand Spades or Bid Whist. We also challenged each other in playing backgammon almost daily, but tennis became one of our favorite activities together.

Although we practiced and played continuously, it came as a surprise when Miss Sue tapped us to be on the junior varsity tennis team. We had come a long way. Before coming to Walker's, neither of us had ever held a tennis racket. We had no tennis equipment, not even balls. We learned how to play the game and developed some mastery on the court. Our communication with each other when we played enhanced our game. And with me as a lefty, we both sides of the court covered with forehand shots.

Dollee often brought home hand-me-down clothes from the white lady whose house she cleaned. Whenever that woman cleaned out her closet, Dollee would see if Jimmie or I could wear the clothes. In junior high school, I wore that woman's black sweater set with her initials monogrammed in tan on the front of the cardigan. Although my first and last names did not begin with "J" or "C," I proudly wore that sweater set. No one ever questioned me about the monogram on the sweater, mainly because no children in our community wore monogrammed clothing.

Miss Sue made it clear that, for the matches, we had to wear tennis whites. I had two sets of tennis whites. One was an outfit that Jimmie and Dollee bought me at Steffy's; the other was a hand-me-down set from the same white woman with the JC initials.

Nyoka and I were about the same size, only I was taller. The Steffy outfit was a child-size set, and we decided that one would be appropriate for her to wear, and I would sport the other one. Unlike the other girls, we did not wear Tretorn tennis shoes, just the same old shoes we wore for volleyball and basketball in the winter. The tennis coach loaned us tennis rackets for the season. Although we didn't possess tennis gear, we had heart and soul and thought we were super bad. Before leaving for our first competitive tennis match, we admired ourselves in the bathroom mirror. I called myself "Veda Ashe" after Arthur Ashe, and Nyoka was "Althea Gibson."

In our first competitive match, we won the first set and lost the last two sets. We came closer to winning our next match, but we lost that one, too. Although discouraged and dismayed, we vowed to continue playing and practicing together.

That spring Coach Scarles posted an announcement about a tennis tournament at Walker's. It was not the first tournament, but it would be the first one that we would enter.

"You think we should sign up?" I asked.

"Why not?" Nyoka replied.

"Who do you think we'll end up playing?"

"Who knows? We can handle whoever we play."

"Oh, really? You have a lot of confidence in us."

"Sure do."

We signed up for the tournament, and lo and behold, we were matched with two players who were on the varsity tennis team. Angela and Valerie had played tennis since they were little kids at their parents' country clubs, and they had skill. Nyoka and I had a lot of nerve. We practiced every day leading up to the match.

Like the professional players, we shook hands at the net before our match. Nyoka played on the right side of the court while I covered the left, thus limiting the number of backhand shots we had to make. We played our hearts out. We used all the skills we had learned up to that point in our tennis classes. The result of the match astonished everyone.

The tournament brackets and scores were posted on the bulletin board just outside of the bookstore. Angela and Valerie posted the scores. To our surprise, lots of girls were anxious to see the results. Even Coach Scarles was curious. Nyoka and I lost, but the scores were 9-7 for the first set, and 8-6 for the second set. It had taken those two seasoned tennis players thirty games to beat us. We were beaten, but not defeated.

"What a match!" Coach Scarles exclaimed. "Who saw that coming?"

"We played our best," I said.

"I bet you did, and it shows here."

Although we had lost again, Nyoka and I had performed extraordinarily well, and we were pleased with ourselves. We had accomplished in that match more than anyone could have ever predicted. In our minds, we were our own tennis champs that day. Angela and Valerie won the entire tournament.

***

As luck would have it, we left the tennis court feeling stronger than ever in our friendship. We were indeed "ever the best of friends." Nothing and no one could come between the love and respect that we held for each other. I had found the true friend I so desperately desired. Nyoka was all she said she would be as my friend. Later that week, I was not the friend she needed, and I'm positive she wasn't sure about me, either.

Nyoka and I did as much as we could together while at Walker's. When the decision came to take a group of seniors on a day trip to Boston, Nyoka and I went together. We sat together on the bus and planned to do the same things. Because ABC was located on Boylston Street in Boston, we took a picture together on that street. We each got a copy of the picture and wrote "ever the best of friends" as the caption. We decided our senior pictures would be adjacent to each other in the senior section of Walker's yearbook. When I went to New York for a break to see Wanda, Nyoka and I often traveled to the city together.

I had learned so much from Nyoka about growing up and about thinking for myself. We talked about our dreams and what we wanted in life. Although she told me I always looked at the world through rose-colored glasses, I still told her my desire to have a house with a white picket fence and children. I even chose the names André Telemachus, Caius Mariah and Autolychus Decembre (a Shakespearean influence) as names for my children. Together, we shared our deepest woes and concerns about our lives and about the world we lived. We wanted better, but neither of us had any real plans or ideas about how we would achieve better. Walker's gave us the classical tools of knowledge we needed, but we lacked the wit usually offered by mentoring adults.

During the week after the tennis match, words were passed between me and Nyoka in front of Kim, Lynn, and Renée in their Beaverbrook room. Who knows what the disagreement was really about? No one knew. The heated verbal exchange became physical, and I struck my friend with my fists. I surprised both of us, and she wept uncontrollably. I had an adrenalin rush that caused that lump to rise again in my throat that made me want to vomit my heart. I hurt my friend, the one who had repeatedly come to my rescue, who had shown me unconditional love, and who had spent countless hours with me playing games, playing tennis, and braiding hair. And as I settled down, all I could feel was shame. I had brought shame upon myself and had inflicted pain upon a dear friend. How could I have done something so horrific?

Lynn and Kim separated us. Nyoka ran from the room crying. Renée followed her. I just stood there huffing and trying to return to the person I had been before the fight. Unfortunately for both of us, the die was cast, and I could never retract that blow. I was ashamed, but how does one fix such a situation? My brain had no clue. I just wanted the impossible---a do-over so I could have responded differently.

Because we were seniors, the younger black girls looked up to us, and I felt as if I had also let them down. Up until that point, I had been a friend and confidante to several of them. I had not behaved as a role model or mentor. And add to it the Christian component, and I had a mess. I had not behaved Christ-like at all.

My shame seeped heavily into my chest, heart, and head like the onset of a summer cold or winter flu. There was no remedy. There was no medicine to heal the situation, or to heal the wound I had inflicted on my dear friend.

Back at Cluett that night, Nyoka closed the sliding door between our rooms. We had lived in that space together for nearly two years and had never shut each other out. This was a first. And while it was painful for me to accept, I had to accept the situation I had created. On the other side of the door, I could hear her softly talking in hushed tones to Robin about the day's events. I felt even more ashamed of what I had done.

That night I sobbed quietly in my pillow. I thought about how awful I had been to someone who genuinely loved me and who had done everything in her power to look out for me. I selfishly wept for the trust lost in our friendship; and I cried because I saw my own lack of control and sinfulness. I had harmed my friend, my one true friend, my biggest supporter. I wanted everything to be different, but I knew only time would heal the hurt I had inflicted on Nyoka. I was truly remorseful.

It would be a few days before Nyoka and I would talk about what happened. I sincerely apologized, and she accepted my apology, but even so, times were different between us. She forgave me, but I'm not sure I ever really forgave myself. Her spirit was much kinder and a lot gentler than mine would ever be. Within a few days of that altercation, we received our yearbooks. Our senior pages faced each other. Here's what she inscribed in my yearbook.

To Veda, as you well know, the year has not been filled with pleasurable memories for you or I—at least that is how I feel. But I know that the best is yet to come for the both of us. (Good things come to those who wait!) To continue writing would become awkward and corny; that's why I'll end this autograph right here. Good luck and if all pursues, we'll remain ever the best of friends. If not, good luck and remember, I'll always be the shoulder that you can cry or lean on. Good luck and loads of happiness. Love forever and a day.

And there it was, forgiveness, something that I so badly needed and yet did not deserve. What a friend! Our relationship had become a committed friendship.

47

Decisions, Decisions

Mrs. Johnson served as both the bookstore manager and as the school's postmaster, so she saw every piece of mail that came to the campus. She knew who got mail from family and friends on a regular basis, and she knew who got into which college. The thickness of the envelope told the story without breaking the seal. Mail was placed in our boxes, and everyone knew what a thin or thick envelope meant.

My first thick envelope came from Briarcliff College, and it was replete with scholarship papers and a commitment letter. I had expected as much from them, so I didn't make a big deal out of it. Other girls who had applied there also got thick envelopes.

Two thin letters arrived for me on the same day about a week later. One was from Duke; the other from Mt. Holyoke. The wind in my sail vanished, and I quickly put away the letters and straightened my face. I talked about it only if someone asked.

"Veda, I see you got some mail today. How's it going?" It was Miss MacDougall.

Darn it, how did she see? I had to remind myself, though, that while she struts, her movements were like little cat's feet, soft, yet deliberate, and she seemed to know what was going on around her.

"I got two rejection letters today, and that's not good. I was accepted at Briarcliff and the University of Arkansas. Briarcliff gave me money, but I haven't heard about money from Arkansas. The thin envelopes were from Duke and Holyoke."

"I'm sorry to hear that. No news from Wesleyan?"

"Not yet. I'm not sure what's taking so long. And I really don't know what to expect. Did you hear Nyoka got into Barnard?"

"Yes, we all heard. That's wonderful."

"I should hear from Wesleyan soon."

Every day I went to the mailroom to check for more mail. The usual letters came from Pine Bluff. It was getting close to graduation, and members of St. Paul had already started sending graduation gifts. Dollee wrote me often. It was always a pleasure to hear from home, but right then, I was awaiting news from colleges.

The folk at Wesleyan took their own sweet time. I didn't dare call and inquire about my application. No one I knew had ever done that. You just waited, and so I did. By that time, Nyoka was also accepted to Hunter College in New York. She was pleased with both acceptance letters and the scholarships they offered. Both institutions had given her full rides.

A few days later, as I was standing in line to check my mail, two other senior hopefuls stood behind me. Mrs. Johnson handed me my mail.

"Looks like you've got some good news," she said.

The thick Wesleyan envelope was on top, and before I could open the letter, the other two seniors screamed.

"Open it! Open it!" they shouted.

I quickly tore open the letter. It read: *"We are pleased to offer you admission to the class of 1979."*

That was it. I smiled with jubilation. The other two seniors ran into the smoking room to announce my good news. I read a little bit more. I had no clue what it would cost me to finish college. No one had had that conversation with me either. No one told me about applying for numerous scholarships or what to think about in making the right decision for college attendance. As I read on, I learned that Wesleyan was indeed offering me a scholarship, a really good scholarship. Tuition, room, and board in 1975 cost about $5,000 each year, and they gave me $4,000 per year. I would have to take out $1,000 each year in student loans. While that may not seem like much, in 1975, $1,000 was a lot of money. And while it wasn't a totally full ride, it was close enough.

As I walked into the dining hall for lunch that day, my classmates serenaded me with the *Hoo-ray Sun-ray* song. Like the other girls who had gotten acceptance letters, I beamed with pride. And although I was proud, I had no clue as to what being accepted to attend Wesleyan meant or the kind of education I might get there.

"So, what's your decision?" Miss MacDougall asked.

"I don't quite know what to do. I haven't made a decision."

"What do you mean?"

"I got a scholarship to go to the University of Arkansas also. If I go there, I won't have any student loans. Everything will be paid for."

"Hmmm. Is that what you want?"

"I'm not sure."

"Do you want to return to Arkansas for college?"

"Not really. I'm just trying to figure out what to do."

"What do you think your brother will say? Will he think you should go there?"

"He said earlier I should go to Wesleyan if I am accepted. He mentioned it being one of the Little Three, also. I'm not sure what that *really* means."

"It means that it's a highly selective school and one that is hard to get into. You've already done the hardest part, and that is getting in. Of the schools you've gotten accepted to, Wesleyan is the most prestigious. The others are just okay, but going to Wesleyan is a big deal. Does that help?"

"Yes, it does help. I will talk to Marion again and Jimmie. She'll be okay with whatever he suggests I should do. I'll do what he thinks is best."

Since he was out of college and working, Marion sent me my $100 deposit to hold my place at Wesleyan. I had decided to attend a college that was only forty-five minutes away from Walker's, but whose campus I had never visited. I had only had the interview with the alumnus, so I hadn't even spoken to anyone other than the admissions counselor at the university. I had so many uncertainties.

Had I made the right decision? Was I ready? Had Walker's truly prepped me for college? What would it be like going to school with boys again? Could I handle that? What about the workload? And what would it mean to get a liberal arts degree? Would I be able to get a job afterwards? Would I have to become a teacher if I majored in English? What did all this mean? Was I prepared socially, emotionally, and academically for Wesleyan? Only time would tell.

***

Senior week at Walker's was packed with activities to create unforgettable memories. Unfortunately, I forgot most of them, since I didn't actively participate in any of them. I was present but not a part. There was a pool party for seniors at a trustee's home. Each girl received Walker's mementos. One was a little glass that looked like a martini glass with the school name and a sundial etched in green on it, and the other was a silver pendant with a purple sundial. School leaders toasted us as we walked around the in-ground pool in flowing dresses. Nyoka and I stayed together and talked to Robin and another girl. We were finally preparing to leave Walker's, a place that held bittersweet memories for each of us. The trustee inducted us into The Ethel Walker Alumnae Association.

Because a classmate had connections, George Plimpton was our graduation speaker. All awards and prizes went to white girls and nice white ladies, a final gentle reminder of our exclusion. We wore long white dresses and carried a bouquet of purple and gold flowers like we were members of a wedding party. LaWanda had my dress made by a seamstress in New York. It was a haltered top with a jacket that tied at the waist. Jimmie, LaWanda, and Buster came for my graduation as did LaWanda's friend Ruth and my cousin Brendia from Indianapolis. To Brendia's surprise, one of my classmates was the daughter of one of her professors at an Indiana university. I wanted Dollee and Mama to come, but my family didn't have the money for that many people to travel to Connecticut.

Walker's hosted a reception for graduates and their families after the ceremony. In effort to avoid tears, when I returned to Cluett to fetch my belongings and depart, I found that Nyoka had already left. We had talked previously about our departure, and she said she did not like goodbyes. We both knew that we would cry if we had to say goodbye to each other in person. Her mom and a friend helped her gather her possessions and leave.

My family helped me get most of my belongings to Ruth's car. I left a few boxes of books and papers that I would return to pick up in the fall. The drive down the hill was solemn. I didn't turn to look back for fear of bad luck. Waving goodbye to the sign at the end of the driveway, we turned left and headed to the airport.

48

Mirror, Mirror

The Latina Uber driver pulled her silver SUV into the drive in front of Beaverbrook. It was my first return visit to The Ethel Walker School since 1975. It had been more than forty years since I last walked on the school grounds. Once again, I arrived at the school alone with my bags. Only this time, I arrived as a grown woman who had managed to rear a family and eke out a career in education. While I was still Veda from Pine Bluff, my life had changed and grown in ways that I could not have imagined when I was a student at Walker's. There I was, in a familiar environment, retracing steps and reminiscing about my time there.

The director of alumni relations met me in the lobby of Beaverbrook just as the women and girls had met me so many years ago. Commencement had occurred two days prior to my visit, so there were few people on campus. As she showed me around the campus, memories were rekindled, both pleasant and not so pleasant; but overall, I decided that my coming to Walker's in 1972 had been the right decision for me. The results of that decision had been reflected in almost every facet of my life, and now I could see clearly through the looking glass what the Walker's experience meant for me. While the initial images that I first saw in the mirrors of Beaverbrook were those of a young black girl, what I now saw were images of an African American woman who had survived the struggle of growing up and learning in a foreign place to become a woman who had begun to recognize her own gifts and talents and to use them in service to others. I was pleased with what I saw.

While at Walker's, I learned how to learn and how to think about how students are taught at different schools. I learned that students at prep schools receive an uncommon education, even with the inequities and biases. The student workload is pitched at a different level, and the underlying assumption about each student is that you want to be there, and you want to learn at high levels. I found that many of the learning experiences I had in the 1970's at Walker's are still unavailable to students in many public schools. I learned that teachers in schools like Walker's are lifelong learners who hone their crafts continuously in hopes of delivering first rate content to their students. They are sacrificially committed to the work that they do in preparing students for college and beyond. For them, it is never about a test score alone, but learning is about helping students to grow and to develop in ways that will allow them to achieve their goals and dreams. Theirs is a commitment to education excellence.

Attending Walker's was a culture shock for me. When I arrived there, I had only gone to school with white people for three years, and not only was I going to school with them, I was living with them and having all of my meals with them. White Simsbury, Connecticut may as well have been in another country. That's what it felt like. I was in a foreign land and required to live as if I had always been a part of that lily-white upper middle-class culture. It was no wonder that the black girls huddled together whenever we had an opportunity to reconnect, to recharge, and to check ourselves. It was our way of staying connected, calibrating, and developing some sort of identity. The expectation was that we would be able to come into the new environment and function like the white girls for whom the school was built. While I was able to demonstrate some academic prowess, I wonder what would have happened had I had the intentional support of capable adults in helping me make decisions and handle the changes I encountered as a young black girl in that environment.

Walker's wanted to give us what we needed, but no one ever bothered to ask us what that need was. No one seemed to realize that perhaps the black students needed something different or something more to support us in our learning and socializing in our environment. Just because we couldn't articulate clearly what we wanted and needed didn't mean we didn't yearn for more – more support, more clarity with goal setting and expectations, more openness about opportunities, and yes, more social and emotional support. It seemed as if they thought all teenage girls needed the same thing. That could not have been further from the truth, but there was no adult to bring that to their attention, and as students, we were not sure what to expect from day to day or how to best articulate our concerns. It became, for me, an exercise in survival, when it should have been an experience that helped me learn how to thrive beyond the walls of Walker's as a black woman in America; but they couldn't give us what they didn't have. And even if they'd had the wherewithal to offer that kind of support, would we have recognized it as support in the 1970's?

The teen years are difficult enough to manage with daily parental guidance. Imagine what it's like without that guidance and adult influence daily. Every decision becomes a challenge when one does not have the insight of a responsible adult speaking into her life. Peers rarely have appropriate responses or insight because they are trying to figure out life, too. Rarely were meaningful conversations held with an adult outside of the classroom. If I wanted to talk to an adult, I had to initiate that interaction.

I wondered how Walker's staff viewed me. At home, Jimmie and Dollee saw my gifts and talents early in my life. My skin color did not matter to them. Before my birth, I was expected to be black because of who my parents were. At Walker's, the reverse was true. They saw my skin color first, and often de-valued and doubted my gifts and talents. At home, I had purpose, value and worth; not so much at Walker's. They were blinded by the conditions of the times, biases—both individual and institutional, and their own agendas for ensuring that the rich white girls got the education that they believed *they* deserved. As a black student, they assumed we would go along to get along. That was not good for us, especially for me since I had come from a vocal home environment where I frequently expressed my thoughts and feelings and acted when necessary.

I have also wondered what parents think and feel will happen to their children when they send them to prep schools. Do they think that school personnel know what's better for their child? Sending a child to such a school includes giving all authority for every aspect of the child's life to someone else. It means someone else will look out for the physical, social, emotional, and academic wellbeing of the child. That's placing a lot of trust in someone else whom you may or may not have met. It's giving the school staff *loco parentis* at a time when a child needs the influence of a parent who knows her best at a critical juncture, namely the teen years.

The question that remained for me was, did Walker's do a better job for me than if I had remained in Pine Bluff? The answer is a resounding "yes." Yes, difficult times occurred, but some of them probably would have happened at any school, considering my personality and the times in which we lived.

I experienced tremendous growth as a learner at Walker's and became a well-read student of the classics. My study habits were nurtured and developed in an environment that encouraged learning and engagement. After procrastinating a few times, I crammed for tests. My writing improved as I took chances on exploring controversial issues even in the face of uncertainty about teacher responses. For three years, I absorbed as much as my brain would hold about a variety of topics, and although initially, I didn't speak up in class, by the time that I left, I had found my voice again and was unafraid to express my views. That was growth.

As a human being, I discovered how I could live with people of all descriptions and other races. I learned how to live communally with other girls. I became skilled at how to look out for myself even when no one else was. And I began to understand that relationships, especially friendships, take a lot of work over time to be meaningful and remain positive. These were all skills I needed going to college, and these experiences both personal and academic prepped me and allowed me to walk onto a college campus with a definite sense of who I was and what I was capable of attaining. And because I experienced success at Walker's, I realized I could achieve goals no matter how difficult.

49

The Rest of the Story

Although our lives took different directions, Jackie and I have continued to be in touch with each other over the years through holiday greetings. On occasion, we have shared a meal when I visited cities near her. We have never discussed what happened in "The Invitation."

Nyoka and I have remained friends since our time at Walker's. She went to Barnard College. At times, we talk more often than at other times. We continue to share our thoughts, dreams, and hopes for our families and for ourselves. She knows more about me as a human being than any other person on the planet because now just as when we were at Walker's, she listens with her heart and her head. I know I can count on her for an honest review of any situation. We have been friends longer than I have been friends with any other person. I will always be grateful for the opportunity to meet her at Walker's.

Kabrian went to the University of Massachusetts-Amherst and returned to California after graduation. After finding out that I was going to Wesleyan, he remarked, "I knew you were smart, but not that smart." His comment affirmed my decision about our relationship.

After graduating from Princeton, Marion enrolled in law school and later Harvard Divinity School. He became a lawyer and a pastor in the Presbyterian Church. While practicing law and pastoring, he became the first African American judge in Arkansas since Reconstruction. Four years later, he became a circuit court judge. I ran his first two campaigns for judge.

Out of curiosity and a desire to reconnect, I answered Martha (Levy) Lehmann's letter with a lengthy email update on my life. I saw it as an opportunity for redemption-redeeming a relationship that didn't happen, but probably should have happened during our time at Walker's together. I wanted to get to know her on a personal level that would be different from what I witnessed at Walker's. Although I didn't think she liked me while at Walker's, I realized we had never taken the time to talk and get to know each other. We never had any meaningful informal conversations outside of class or shared a meal. It had only been a formal teacher-student relationship. We knew virtually nothing about each other.

She responded to my email, and a friendship ensued. I wasn't sure what to call her, at first. Neither name, Mrs. Levy nor Ms. Lehmann (a return to her birth name) seemed right, so I asked. She insisted I call her by her first name, so I did.

Our friendship took off in a pleasant direction. For the years that followed the arrival of her letter, we found ways to grow as friends and get to know each other. Both of us suffered major losses of loved ones to cancer. I lost my mother in 2008, and she lost her only son two years later.

We have supported each other and talked about a range of interesting topics, especially equity, social justice, and race relations in America. Neither of us has all the answers, but at least we can talk about black and white issues. She has offered wise counsel at difficult times, and I have listened with my heart to her concerns.

Although we were at Walker's at the same time, our experiences and perspectives differed greatly. She was a young, white teacher learning the ropes of teaching, and I was a young black girl who was new to everything at the school. We were different, but the love of learning and books connected us. Time and space put us there at the same time, not by accident, but purely by design to help both of us become who we would become as friends.

Both of us read so we talk about books we've read and make book suggestions. We email each other often and talk by telephone like old friends. We have each visited the other in her home, and Martha even attended my youngest child's college graduation. Who knew in 1972 that we would ever be friends and share details of our lives with each other? Life stories are sometimes funny in how they are knitted together over time, space, and place. I thought when I left Walker's, I would never see her again. Little did I know she would become an integral part of my life years later as our friendship blossomed and matured.

Perhaps time and space had changed our lives in ways neither of us had imagined.

50

I Am From – Part II

I am from a big afro, pink sponge curlers, cornrows, and balcony singing...

...from wool argyle socks, pastel uniforms, and Bass Weejuns.

I am from the immaculate 800-acre campus, tennis courts, soccer fields, and riding rinks...

...green, cozy, breathtaking, and well-manicured.

I am from dogwoods, crepe myrtles, maple trees, and knee-deep snow...

...blooming, turning, and falling before winter.

I'm from the new girl/old girl show, plays, Lacunas, concerts, jams, suns, and dials...

…from Jimmie, Dollee, nice white ladies, house parents, and drivers.

I'm from the Soul Train line, tennis matches, basketball games, and ice hockey, too…

…from think for yourself and think more of yourself.

I'm from a faith that would not shrink and Sunday afternoon chapel.

I'm from Pine Bluff and Simsbury…

…turnip greens, wax beans, butternut squash, and coffee ice cream.

The quiet voice that grew louder and assertive with time.

Yearbooks, sticky photo albums, and picture boxes.

Chronicling a time, a life, a place of preparation.

Veda in ninth grade

Veda at ABC
Summer Program
at Williams
College 1972

Article from The Pine Bluff Commercial, March 1972, announcing the scholarship

Jimmie and Dollee share a laugh.

Rosie Drew "Mama" Pendleton and
Doris "Dollee" Pendleton ready for
church

Thanksgi
ving 1972
visiting
LaWanda
on Staten
Island

Christmas
1972 in Pine
Bluff with
LaWanda
and Buster

Hot pants and a haltered top at the Choate Rosemary Hall Jam 1973

Veda's fresh afro at Christmas 1972

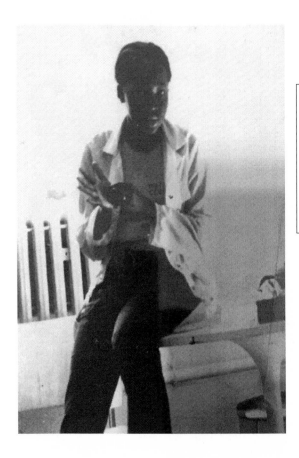

Outside
the
smoking
room
during
milk
lunch

Dining Hall lunch
at Beaverbrook

Easter 1973 on Staten Island

Veda sitting on the fence at the Walker's hockey field

Study hall in a
Hotchkiss shirt

In front of
Beaverbrook
1974

Having fun
babysitting Tammie

Veda and
LaWanda
on Staten
Island 1974

Smiling
for the
camera
outside
Cluett
Hall 1974

Posing inside the
courtyard at
Cluett Hall 1975

Senior Pictures
1974 – 1975 at
Cluett Hall

A Finishing Touch For School Fashions

Veda Pendleton has chosen to continue her spring studies at Ethel Walker School at Simsbury, Connecticut, in this three-piece ensemble in black and white. Her plaid "baggy" pants feature wide cuffs and a zipper up the front. A white knit crop top with black trim adds a frilly look and a corduroy jacket in black completes her ensemble. Miss Pendleton is the daughter of Mrs. Jimmie Pendleton of 913 East 19th Avenue.

Modeling an outfit for The Pine Bluff Commercial

288

Area School News

CAMBRIDGE, Massachusetts — Marion A. Humphrey, 25, son of Mrs. Doris L. Pendleton of 913 East 19th Avenue, Pine Bluff, has been awarded a $4,385 grant to attend Harvard University Divinity School here, according to an announcement from the school.

Humphrey is a 1972 graduate of Princeton (New Jersey) University and has studied at the University of Arkansas Law School at Fayetteville.

He is a former reporter for The Commercial and has served as a summer intern to former Senator J. William Fulbright of Fayetteville and as an intern for Congresswoman Shirley Chisholm, Democrat of New York. He is a member of St. Paul Baptist Church in Pine Bluff.

•

MIDDLETOWN, Connecticut — Veda Pendleton, 18, daughter of Mrs. Jimmie L. Pendleton of 913 East 19th Avenue, Pine Bluff, has received a $4,200 grant to attend Wesleyan University here next fall, the school announced.

Miss Pendleton now is a student at Ethel Walker School in Simsbury, Connecticut, where she is president of the Black Student Union and the Athletic Association. She also serves as a dormitory representative and participates in track, tennis and basketball.

MARION A. HUMPHREY   VEDA PENDLETON

Article announcing my scholarship to attend Wesleyan University and Marion's scholarship to attend Harvard.

Afterword

"I am so sorry to hear of your mother's passing," I said over the telephone.

"Thanks, Veda. She was a good patient, and she planned a lot."

I called Mrs. Broughton's son, Stephen, a respected psychiatrist in Pine Bluff, to express my condolences upon her death. A public school librarian for over forty years, she impacted countless lives, including mine. Our conversation that day quickly turned to our time together as students in junior high school and my departure for prep school. We talked for over an hour mostly about other gifted and talented black students in Pine Bluff in the 1970's and how those students were treated at Pine Bluff High School after I left. I was intrigued by his interest in my prep school experience. Although he would have been an ideal ABC student, his mother decided her only child would not attend prep school.

A few days later, Buster relayed to me comments made by one of his friends. An accomplished retired military man, Benjamin Frazier, said, "I was so proud of Veda when she went to prep school. I felt like she told Pine Bluff 'Take that!'" I pondered his comments. He later told me he has been proud of me for many years.

As a teen, I never gave any thought to what my departure for prep school meant for anyone else in our community, especially my peers. I thought it was only for me, yet, others were watching and found pride in my presence at Walker's. The comments of these two men became the impetus for this book.

It was uncommon in the 1970's for poor black families to send their teenage children out into the world away from home to attend a boarding school. Although Marion had gone to Exeter, he was a male child who was older when he ventured away from home. Attending prep school in the North was still unusual for a black southern child. The decision to let me attend The Ethel Walker School had to cost Jimmie and Dollee a great deal of concern. It took a lot of trust and courage on their part to let me go. As a child, I had no idea what it all meant. I knew I would be going someplace special, learning new material, and discovering something more about myself. I can only imagine the questions and the concerns they must have had about my whereabouts.

They must have had confidence in me, too. I was a talker, and one thing they could always count on was my willingness to tell the truth and to tell everything about any and all of it. They knew I would come home and tell it like it was. They undoubtedly heard some of the stories I have shared here, but not all of them. While these stories mattered to me a great deal, they were less significant to them. Jimmie and Dollee wanted to be assured that I was safe and well. And although they didn't know the adults who were in charge, they trusted that those strangers would look out for me and make decisions that were in my best interest. That was more often the case than not during my time at Walker's.

Oftentimes, education administrators want to simply throw money at students of color to lure them to their institutions and programs. My Walker's experience taught me that economically disadvantaged students usually need more than just the financial assistance to experience meaningful classroom engagement and successful outcomes. All teens struggle with growing up and experience angst, but the struggle is intensified in environments that do not have in place intentional diversity, equity, and inclusion policies and practices to meet the learning, social, and emotional needs of each and every student, especially students of color.

Students who are like me desire mentoring and effective guidance that will usher them through the daily challenges posed in adjusting academically, socially, and emotionally. Money is never the only need; students need love, a sense of belonging, and support both inside and outside of the classroom. Love in the curriculum is social justice—social justice readings, discussions and assignments that help all students grow and learn in meaningful ways that will transform their lives.

I don't know if prep school is what every child needs, but these schools offer a level of preparation that's often not available to students, especially students of color, in public schools. Prep schools open a different world for their students. The mere exposure to students who come from all over the world is a lesson in cultural differences, similarities, and acceptance that is often not experienced in many public schools. The shared and communal living spaces of boarding schools allow for the development of deep relationships that can last for decades. And the individual personal growth that takes place prepares students for the college years ahead of their peers who do not attend a boarding school. My Walker's experience helped me close academic gaps in what to expect in college and beyond. The academic rigor of the work I had at Walker's remained unmatched until I entered a graduate program many years later.

Many think that children come to school with no learning, but every child comes to school with some understanding about the world in which she inhabits. She knows what she has seen and been taught in her home, even if some of her learning is vicarious. She knows something. Teachers just have to figure out what it is that she knows and use that information to determine future instruction and learning.

Researchers talk about the notion that economically disadvantaged children do not perform academically at the same rates as their more affluent peers because of a lack of exposure to books and an enriched vocabulary. I have never believed that notion. Dollee and Jimmie talked to us about school and getting an education. My aunt read the Bible to us each morning, and they took us to places so that we could see local attractions and be exposed to what our community had to offer. No, we did not have personal libraries stocked with children's books, but our family subscribed to the local newspaper, owned a set of World Book encyclopedias, and we watched the evening news nightly. We listened to Walter Cronkite on CBS and kept up with local news by reading *The Pine Bluff Commercial*. Because the owners of the newspaper and an award-winning editor at the newspaper were Jewish, the lead story most days was about Israel. These experiences, while less than what education researchers say economically disadvantaged children need, were what I needed to prepare me for schooling beyond Pine Bluff.

As a young girl, I was prepped for future living as a black female in America, understanding many of the challenges I would face in getting an education and earning a living in this society. I was prepared to develop some sense of independence and facility with learning. I was taught to believe in my own capabilities and to regard myself as a thinker, problem solver, and successful human being.

I was also prepared to live in a world of differences and to be open both internally and externally to a variety of experiences. I was challenged to think differently about myself as a human being even when I didn't always like what I saw in myself. I was challenged to re-examine my own thoughts, motives, and actions. I was also prepped to think about the actions of others and about how I must choose my response to their actions. Through it all, I learned about the value of understanding human frailty and offering forgiveness.

I was prepped to read a variety of works, even if the protagonists were not like me, and to develop an appreciation for what these authors had written. I was prepped to explore and to learn different ideas about what it means to live in this country and interact on personal and professional levels with folks who may or may not look like me or think and behave as I do.

What Walker's did not teach me was how to succeed as a black woman in America in all the arenas I would dare to enter. At that time, they did not invest in the staff, faculty, or curricular resources which could help me do that. That was by design. Ethel Walker planned and designed the school with wealthy white girls in mind and not girls like me. I don't know if she was opposed to having black girls at her school or not, but there was no evidence in the school's curriculum, or otherwise, that we were ever a consideration or that we were valued and belonged at the school. Fortunately, for me, I had models in Jimmie and Dollee, who talked to me about the struggles of being black in America, and models in our church, who embodied all that a black woman could become.

And although my journey to Walker's was a culture shock, I would not trade that journey for anything. It was what I needed, and therefore, worth every step and misstep, every lesson, every page I read, every pain I experienced, and every friendship cultivated. I am grateful for every minute of my Walker's preparation, but I am most appreciative of the preparation of the home training I got from Jimmie and Dollee.

Book Discussion Questions

1. In what ways did Veda's learning in Pine Bluff prepare her for life at The Ethel Walker School? Discuss specifics mentioned in her early life.

2. Veda talks about Jimmie and Dollee throughout her story. What roles did they play in her success?

3. Learning how to travel alone was important to Veda early in her life. How did knowing how to travel alone impact her journey to Walker's? What character traits did traveling alone develop in her?

4. Think about the injustices Veda endured. How could they have been handled differently? How and why do students experience similar injustices today?

5. Revisit the relationships Veda had with her teachers in Pine Bluff and at Walker's. How were they similar? In what ways were they different?

6. To what degree do white teachers know how to meet the academic needs of each and every student, especially gifted students of color?

7. Although Veda was physically included in the classes at Walker's, how could classroom practices have been conducted differently to give greater meaning to her and help her experience success?

8. Veda struggled initially with some of the relationships she had with other black girls. How did her friendship with Nyoka and her relationship with Kabrian help her remain at Walker's?

9. How do you think Veda's Walker's experience helped her grow as a young black woman in America?

10. What are the larger messages in Veda's story about education and gifted students of color?

About the Author

Dr. D. Veda Pendleton grew up in Pine Bluff, AR, in the 1960's and 1970's when African American families prepared their children for the racially charged and segregated America they would encounter beyond the confines of their homes. It was the era of the Civil Rights Movement, and families like hers knew their daughters and sons needed to be prepared to face not only the rigors of learning at high levels, but also the racism and biases that accompanied life in America for people of color. *Prepped: Coming of Age in Black and White America* is her first memoir and her fifth book. She has previously written about parenting her five children and about education.

Dr. Pendleton is an educator. She lives and writes in Louisville, KY. Her degrees are from Wesleyan University, University of Central Arkansas, and The University of Georgia. She has five adult children and seven grandchildren. The Sensational Seven visit her for Cousins Camp each summer.

Read more about her at www.vedapendleton.com .

Other Books by the Author

Written under the name Veda Pendleton McClain

I Mastered Parenting, and Here's What I Did, Parenting Strategies That Work (2016)

All Your Words Are True, Reminders of God's Promises (2014)

Your Presence Is Requested; Critical Essays on Parenting and Education (2013)

The Intentional Parenting Plan (2009)